Two,
If By Van

Best wishes on all your travels,
Karen McGinnis

Karen McGinnis

Copyright©2009 Set to Sell Publishing. All rights reserved.

Published in the United States by Set to Sell Publishing.

ISBN 978-0-9814776-0-2

Distributed by: Set to Sell Publishing, 2805 Kauhale St., Kihei, HI 96753

LCCN   PCN # 2009901600

First Edition
Printed in the Untied States
9 8 7 6 5 4 3 2 1

Dedication

This book is dedicated to my husband, Steve Frayer for whom a road trip through Mexico, Central American and South America was a part of his life-long process of seeing the world. Including me in his dream made the experience of the trip a part of my life as well, and expanded my horizons. This book is also dedicated to my son, Michael Seadler, whose independence allowed me to step out of my everyday life and into the unknown.

About the Author

The author is a graduate of Westmont College with a degree in English Literature and a teaching credential. A senior trip to England, Europe, the Mediterranean and Israel first opened the window on travel. Through this window, she glimpsed the opportunities for adventure and growth that were a benefit of the travel experience.

As a wife and mother, she spent many years at 'home' in California where she taught school, ran a Real Estate company and a design business while participating in community activities. She put her writing skills to work producing marketing pieces, writing advertising copy and creating learning experiences for students who ranged from birth to 80 years of age.

Besides jobs for pay, she served as a board member on the local Chamber of Commerce, the Board of Realtors and the Santa Cruz County Visitor and Convention Bureau. She was a member of the local chapter of Soroptomists International. She supported the local hospital foundation as project coordinator for fundraising. During this time she received awards for volunteer of the year, and several sales recognitions from the Board of Realtors.

When the trip chronicled in this book presented itself through an offer from future husband Steve Frayer, she sold a series of travel articles based on the trip to the local paper, The Santa Cruz Sentinel. After resigning her teaching job, paying bills a year in advance and renting her house to her son, she hit the road in search of adventure and personal growth. The rest is history and is recorded in this book.

Table of Contents

Part I Mexico and Central America

1   Just the Beginning
2   Meeting Pipsqueak and La Dueña
3   Waking Up in a Lake
Map of Mexico
4   Attack of the Body Snatchers
5   A Hellish Night and the Morning After
6   The Beautiful Road
7   What We Had Learned So Far
8   Home Away From Home
9   Coast to Coast: Touching Mexico
Map of Central America
10   Getting Peeped
11   Learning About "Good Enough"
12   The Colors of Belize
13   On the Water in Belize
14   The Border Game
15   The Shores of Lake Yaxha
16   A Garret in Guatemala
17   On the Rio Dulce
18   The Start of the Ruta Maya
Map of the Ruta Maya
19   The End of the Ruta Maya
20   Safe Camping
21   A Different Story
22   Lost in the Mist
23   Wind God of the Rincon
24   How to Ship a Van

Table of Contents, Continued

Part II South America

25	A Walking Tour of Quito
26	Everybody Needs a Bus Monkey
27	Retrieving a Van
28	The First Eight Days in Peru
29	Organization in the Sand
30	Death on a Bus
31	Poor Man's Galapagos
32	Where Condors Soar
33	Taking a Break from the Van
34	The Skin of the Atacama
35	The Smell of Time
36	Memories of Tastes and Smells
37	A Visit to the Lake Country
38	Crossing the Continent
39	Visiting the 50's
40	Fire and Ice
41	On the Icy Trail
42	Learning to Drink Maté
43	Virtually Real Driving
44	Somewhere In Between
45	Copacabana
46	Wet and Dry and Sandy
47	Water World
48	The Beginning of the End
49	Leaving It All Behind
50	Home Again, Home Again

Map of South America

"*The most incomprehensible thing about the world is that it is comprehensible.*"

Albert Einstein

Chapter 1

Just the Beginning

We haven't even left the driveway, and already the adventure has begun. Just loading a 20 year old VW camper van for a 10 month, 15,000 mile trip is a test of your determination, creativity, and patience! Our cultural, spiritual and language exploration of Central and South America is just that kind of a test.

Why would anyone take this kind of a trip? I was feeling settled, and while not bored, somewhat boring. This trip was a chance to be unsettled and challenged, certainly anything but bored or boring. Steve was suffering from itchy feet. I guess we were just in the right place and right time of our lives to do it. Timing is everything.

I was a teacher/realtor/designer from a small town in California. Divorced with one son of legal and independent age, I saw a trip like this one as a chance to make a break from everything ordinary. It was an opportunity to test personal boundaries and abilities, and a chance to reevaluate how I saw the world. It was a shake down trip to see if the new year-old relationship with Steve would endure.

Steve, at 40, was never married, never settled, living free, no children, no ties and no one to be accountable to except himself. His world was certainly different from mine. He had no real need for luxuries like a flush toilet or for imagined certainties like a door with locks. Steve saw this trip as an opportunity to see if the new relationship with me would endure in the face of traveling, Steve-style. It was a relationship shake down trip for him as well.

Who is to say which of our lifestyles was better, which was more functional? Both were valid, but each was so very different from the other. Circumstances had created our past. Now a trip filled with new, shared experiences would create our future.

Steve was educated as an engineer at a Michigan university. The son of an engineer and the brother of engineers, he was still the odd-man-out in his family. Following college graduation he took off to see the world. He visited Alaska and built log cabins. He studied solar technology in the Rocky Mountains and then drove across the United States on a motorcycle with a dog as a passenger, faithful, but hanging on for dear life. While his peers were settling in to life at home, Steve signed on for 2 years in Togo, West Africa with the Peace Corps. There, as Tchammba (Sir), he helped address the deforestation of the area by introducing fuel conserving stoves that could be built by residents out of the local mud. Amusingly, the new mud stoves were a great advantage to the beer making process in the area. An additional year as an instructor and then a year crossing the

Just the Beginning

African continent, including the Sahara by motorcycle, completed his African experience.

Steve continued on with solar work in California, construction projects in Tonga, study in ashrams in India, backpacking in Nepal, bicycling in Burma, feeding the blood-sucking leeches in Borneo: you should be getting the mental picture of his life by now. Those stories have all been lived, but are not yet written.

While that wild ride occupied Steve, I was experiencing the other side of life. I married soon after graduating college with a teaching degree and settled into life as the wife of a contractor. After moving 17 times in 15 years and giving birth to one child, stress overcame me and divorce followed. Surviving as a single mom and raising a son elevated my level of perseverance. I learned not to give up. That "stay with it" attitude would come in handy on the trip ahead.

I had been raised as a more-or-less only child in a quiet upper middle class household. I had a fear of the unknown and the noisy. That fear was countered by a desire to see the other ways in which people lived. I was used to tip-toeing up to the line of rebellion, but never stepping over. This trip to the end of the world was a step across the line, a statement of independence from parents, off-spring, and ex-husbands. It was a leap into a world I had never imagined. That small feeling of fear never really left the pit of my stomach. I did learn not to think about it, and just press on.

So with our pasts firmly packed away in our personalities, we embarked on a trip of discovery. We would discover not only the world that waited for us in Central and South

America, but also the possibilities and limitations that lay within our selves.

Just what do you take for a trip that will pass through deserts, tropical rainforests, rugged mountain ranges, and ice-choked fjords? Warm clothes and clothes for hot, muggy weather? Sandals and hiking boots and Uggs? Bathing suits and down jackets?

It seems pretty straightforward until you consider that your "space available" to pack this variety of wearing apparel is as big as one dresser drawer. Out goes anything that requires ironing. Out goes anything that can't be mixed-and-matched and layered with everything else. That narrows down the wardrobe to items that will surely be rags by the time we rolled our home on wheels back onto American soil.

What clothes should I take?

Sandals: flat soled, Velcro, water proof or quick drying for walking in streams and taking showers in horrible shower stalls or on mud floors
Hiking boots: broken in, cleanable
Tennis shoes: dark colored to hide dirt
Some kind of semi-dressy shoes that might work at a hotel dining room
Long pants that unzip to form shorts and are made of material that dries quickly, not jeans
Shorts: 2-3 pairs that wash easily, are colorfast and dry fast
1 long sleeved shirt: button front, vented back, fast drying
1 long sleeved shirt: pull over, colorfast
3 T-shirts: colorfast, easy wash, fast drying, dark colored
3 tank tops or sleeveless shirts: easy wash, dark colored, colorfast
One dress-up outfit: washable, non-wrinkling
One loose dress for women for extra hot days, after showers, beach and cultural events
Enough underwear for 1 week: easy wash, sturdy and fast drying
One pair tights or bicycle pants to layer under pants for warmth
Socks: medium to dark colored, 3 light weights, 3 medium weights
Heavy jacket that squeezes up into a small stuff sack: Fiber-fill, washable, quick drying, hooded
Light weight jacket: water repellant, stuff-able, and a sweatshirt, zip front, hooded
Visor, sunhat: foldable and washable, and sun glasses

Q. What should I remember about clothing for a long trip?
A. Everything should be able to mix-and-match with everything else. Layer clothes to address temperature changes. Some days start off cold then progress to hot. Being able to strip off layers and un-zip pant legs saves time and packing space.

Do not take anything you can't afford to loose or have stolen or get ruined. Some small villages do not have laundromats or even electric washing machines and clothes may be washed on rocks (literally) by hand in water that is contaminated. They will still be returned to you by the local laundress cleaner than when you dropped them off at her house. Fragile clothes will not survive that kind of treatment.

Q. What about washing my clothes?
A. Anything that is not colorfast will turn everything else you own a shade of that color. Where there are washers, clothes tend to be dumped into one washer, washed on hot with stinky detergent, then dried on hot with even stinkier perfumed dryer additives. If you have allergies to perfume, be forewarned. Take your own detergent and give it to the laundry. **ASK** for no perfume in the dryer. We had clothes come back to us so smelly that we had to hang them outside the van at night because there was no sleeping with that smell around.

Q. Will my clothes last through the whole trip?
A. Be prepared for your clothes to wear out or break down. Take a needle and thread for quick repairs. Take some extra buttons and Velcro to make things somewhat functional.

Just the Beginning

Q. Can I just shop on the road for new clothes?
A. Some small towns have NO STORES. Shopping does not exist as we know it. The locals wear the same shirt for months or longer and are happy to have it. You will learn to value the clothes on your back. If you find you are not wearing some item of clothing because it is not comfortable or functional or is no longer needed, get rid of it. Bigger towns do have clothing stores of one 'fashion' or another. Give the clothing you don't need to a local person or donate it to a church. The space is more valuable than the clothing.

Another necessity is food. What to take, how to carry it, prepare it, cook it, what to eat it on? Let's see...one pan, one skillet, a propane stove, and let's apply that mix-and-match theory again.

Can you mix the couscous with the tuna? How about the polenta with the sardines in spicy tomato sauce? It may not sound too appetizing when a bounty of epicurean delights are within reach and take-out is even closer, but our experience proved that ANYTHING tastes great when you are hungry, cold, or just miles away from other options.

FAQS
Q. What should I take to meet minimum requirements for food and water?
A. Everyone's dietary needs are different. Here are some suggestions:
Dry food: pasta, flour, sugar in sealed plastic ware. Salt, pepper, dried garlic and onion powders, cereals in zip-lock bags, oatmeal in paper packets, rice and rice meals in packets, couscous, crackers, sauces in flat packets (add

water), dry drink mixes to add to your own filtered water, dry cocoa mixes, teas, coffee, rejuvenation drink powders such as Gatorade, etc. for re-hydration, powdered milk, coffee creamers, pancake mix.
Canned food: Canned meats, soups, vegetables, chilies, meat meals.
Fresh food: Purchase as you go from local markets and stores. Remember that you need to wash in filtered water, peel whenever possible, and cook thoroughly.
Liquids: Juices if in compact containers, 'eternal' milk, rejuvenation fluids such as Gatorade, liquid mineral replacement drinks, etc., oil (small bottle repacked inside a zip lock bag), flavor enhancers such as chili sauce, soy sauce, syrup, etc.

Q. Should I eat my "brought-along food" right away?
A. Your "brought-along food" should be considered special treats or emergency rations. There is never enough room to pack food for a year. Things you just can't live without should also be included in your supplies. For day-to-day, there is food along the way that can be purchased that is similar in substance if not in taste. It will sustain you and expand your horizons and appreciation of things known and unknown.

Q. How should I pack my food?
A. All food items should fit into a plastic bin that can be latched shut. This will guard against insects, rodents, mold and water. Only take what you can pack easily. Only take what you will really eat. Some things are impossible to find in parts of the Third World.

Just the Beginning

Q. Is there anything I may not be able to find on the road?
A. The re-hydration powders and anything other than basic food is available only in big cities. You may not be able to find such basics as bread in some small towns. We often felt lucky to find small hard rolls with which to make sandwiches.

Q. What about eating local food?
A. The local people eat very basic diets of rice, beans, chicken, tortillas and some local vegetables such as peppers and tomatoes. Local vegetables and fruits should be eaten with care. Wash in filtered water. Washing in local tap water is not cleaning anything, but may be adding contaminants.

Q. What about water? Is it safe?
A. We took a ceramic water filtering system with us and at times had to produce a jug of filtered water by hand. We stocked up on filtered water when in larger towns, replenishing our 3 gallon jug which had a tap for daily access and filling all our drinking containers.

Q. How can I keep food cold?
A. We kept fresh foods chilled in a battery run ice chest which was attached to an extra rechargeable battery in the van. Buying ice as you go for an ice chest is counter-productive and just plain frustrating. You begin to focus on your next ice purchase rather than the trip itself.

Q. Is street food safe?
A. Eating at street side food stalls or roadside venders is adventurous, convenient, but risky. Obviously if they

have no running water to wash their hands or implements, their level of cleanliness is suspect. Roadside restaurants often have no running water at all. They are washing their cooking utensils and surfaces with their own local water, something you would not drink directly, but are then getting indirectly through the food. We were very careful about what we ate and where. It is no fun being sick on the road. The two times I got sick were from obvious sources. The first was in Peru from a raw fish *cerviche*. The second was from a roadside restaurant in Ecuador that had absolutely no sanitation at all. Both instances gave me a week of intense illness. The re-hydration mixes and liquids may save your life at times like that.

See box referring to Health Concerns for more information about staying healthy on the road.

Now for the biggest challenge of all. That's right, the challenge of keeping your 20-year old VW alive. Spare parts become the order of the day, but which spare parts are the most crucial?

We purchased guide books and the mechanic's manuals, and the lists begin to grow. Gaskets, pumps, filters, fluids of every description, and all the tools necessary to install, repair or replace anything that may vibrate off and fall, unnoticed, on the washboard roads (or *ripio*) and speed bumps (or *topes*) of Latin America.

Steve worked his way through lists of parts and repairs and check-ups that would help to keep our 1980 VW van on the road and functional throughout the trip through Mexico, Central America and South America. He crossed off things he had accomplished as he made his way methodically

Just the Beginning

through the lists. The energy in the cross-outs gives some impression of his mindset during this process. Driving a not-so-new car has advantages and disadvantages. You are safer from car theft but more at risk from breakdowns. Toss a coin and see which way you want to go. A lot depends on your mechanical abilities and your patience level when under stress.

This is a typical page from Steve's "to do" list as he was getting the van ready to go.

Even on what seems like a deserted road, the next passerby will probably stop to help you if you are stranded. He might even possess mechanical ingenuity, even ability. Life in the Third World demands that cars be kept repaired with or without the right parts. Creativity reaches new levels when necessity is the mother of invention. You might benefit from this ability to "make do". Based on fuel costs and durability, Steve recommends diesel powered vehicles, which he did not have on this trip.

Feeling stressed yet? Reconsidering the wisdom of taking the trip at all? Just a little testy with your travel companion(s) over who takes what and where-in-the-heck are we going to put it? Congratulations. You've crossed the threshold from just thinking about such a trip, which is as far as most people get, and entered the reality of preparing for a major road trip into the mostly unknown.

It can be done. Soon we were on the road for just such a trip, packed to capacity, but still speaking to each other, and, miracle of miracles, we could still see the *floor* of the van.

FAQS
Q. How should I prepare myself to stay healthy on a long trip?
A. If you are a normal, cautious person, you may wish to visit a doctor specializing in travel medicine as you prepare for your extended trip. He will need to know what countries you will be visiting and what shots you have had and when. His office will issue you a Health Card which is a log of all the shots you have had before leaving the United

Just the Beginning

States. Some countries indicate that they need this card before allowing you to enter. This is interesting as most of the residents of these countries have not had the shots that are required to enter the country. I can only assume that this is the country's way of ensuring that you do not become ill while visiting them. They are often not as concerned about the health needs of their own citizens or able to meet their needs due to logistics and finances.

Q. How can I find out more about illnesses to watch out for?
A. There are so many strange illnesses that occur in other countries that there is not enough room in this book to catalogue them all. Visit the web sites for the specific country or the World Health Organization web site (www.who.int) to research what you might encounter.

- ✓ Generally a tetanus shot is an excellent idea. You will no doubt step on or in something that pierces the skin while on your trip.

- ✓ Hepatitis series are also recommended. There are several types. Refer to web sites for requirements. Ask your travel doctor.

- ✓ Gamma Globulin shots are not required, but can add peace of mind as they tend to boost the immune system.

Q. What about my prescriptions?
A. If you are taking any permanent medications including contraceptives or allergy medications, I would recommend taking a supply sufficient to cover the time you will be traveling. Be sure to take the

prescription with you for the border inspections and in case you need to refill your prescription on the road.

BEWARE: If the medication purchased at a pharmacy is not the *exact* type and dosage, it may not even be close to what you should be taking. There have been horror stories of travelers who took medication that was 'close' to their prescription according to local pharmacists and then had complications that required hospitalization or worse!

Q. What else can I do to prepare for my trip?
A. Here are some things to think about. Consider boosting the health of your intestinal tract by eating yogurt or taking alfalfa tablets before and during your trip. A healthy immune system supported by a functioning digestive tract is your best defense against illness.

Watch the water, raw foods, vegetables, and fruit that you eat. If you can't cook it, wash it, peel it, or purify it, don't eat it. Our sanitized American environment has not prepared your system to deal with the many organisms that exist in the Third World.

Stay hydrated.
Get plenty of rest.
Don't eat, drink or party to excess.

And watch your back. I am not only referring to your physical back, but figuratively as well. While you will feel welcomed and at home in most environments, you are not really at home. You are a visitor in someone else's country. Keep that in mind and tread lightly.

Just the Beginning

This doesn't all sound like fun, but preparing yourself in advance and remembering to observe precautions may bring you home healthy and ensure that your trip is enjoyable.

Some travelers prepare for their physical and medical needs, but are surprised when things go wrong on the road.

**Q. How can I stay safe while on a long trip?
A. Keep your eyes and ears open, look, listen and appreciate!**
One recommendation for staying safe on your extended trip is to remember that you are going for the journey, the experience. Do not take anything that you could not easily leave behind, give away, or have stolen. This will free your mind to enjoy the experience and not worry about your "things."

- Stay away from crowded, rowdy situations. If you see a mob forming, find a quiet, safe place at a distance to observe. This is their country and they don't need you in the middle of their demonstration. If the country seems to be heading for anarchy, leave.
- Keep a low profile. Don't wear jewelry or fancy clothes. Dress down. Keep your voice and observations to yourself and your partner. The locals don't need to be addressed by your sense of right and wrong in their own culture. Don't carry fancy cameras, watches, lap tops, or CD players. It may be normal for you, but may represent an overwhelming temptation to someone who has nothing and envisions this as the one opportunity that might present itself to get something.

- Wear a money belt inside your pants or around your neck or both. Don't keep all your money in one place. Don't loose your passport and identification. They are replaceable, but not easily. Take copies of all your important papers and leave copies with loved ones at home, hidden deep within your luggage and in an easily accessible place in your clothing. The copies may be shown to anyone questioning you and be enough to satisfy their interest in just who you are and why you are where you are. Without copies and depending on where you are when they are lost, you may face a long journey to a consulate without papers of any kind.
- You are easily lost and not easily found by loved ones thousands of miles away. No one will remember seeing you or will accurately know where you are now. You must take care of yourself. If someone holds you up for your money, give it to them and hope that that is all that you loose. If you are not in the wrong place at the wrong time, the incidence of robbery diminishes.
- Be aware. Look around. Are there people in the area who look like they are watching you? They probably are. Don't set yourself up to be a victim. There are teams of muggers in crowded markets that separate you from your traveling companions, attempt to pick your pocket, and then act offended if you confront them. Stay with your companions. Keep your jacket closed, important items such as cameras on the inside of your jacket, and don't immediately put your hand on your money if you feel threatened. That just gives the thief the information he needs to pick that exact pocket.

Just the Beginning

- Shop around when making purchases. You don't know the money very well and the market rate even less. If you see the item you want at two or three places, it's guaranteed the prices will be different at each place. Ask if they will take less. Bargain with courtesy and respect.
- Be patient at border crossings and traffic stops. Don't offer to pay a bribe. It may be illegal and get you into more trouble. Cooperate, but be prepared to 'play dumb' and don't give away that you speak the language until you really need it.
- Better to understand what is being said and have the luxury of observing the conversation than being intimidated into paying a bribe. If things get tough, ask to be taken to the 'office' and speak to the 'boss'. Many threatening situations just dissolve at that request.
- Don't be aggressive or confrontational. You can expect to be treated with respect and communicate that with your body language and courtesy. You can expect to be taken advantage of, so keep your eyes open and your mind alert. When you spot a scam, quietly disagree, express disinterest in the options offered to you and watch what happens. It will amaze you how quickly the stories will change, the options will expand and the prices will adjust. Don't be offended by these changes. They are probably culturally acceptable. Remember, you are the visitor in their culture.

"There is no human problem which could not be solved if people would simply do as I advise."
                                                    Gore Vidal

Chapter 2

Meeting Pipsqueak and *La Dueña*

We pulled into the dirt driveway at *Cascabela* Resort just about dusk.

"Are we too late? The place looks deserted?" I expressed the anxiousness that we both felt arriving at an apparently empty campground. We were tired, it was hot, we had no A/C and it would soon be dark.

"Maybe this isn't even the gate. Let's try that driveway up the road." Steve, always interested in preciseness and never wanting to offend, drove ahead to the next dirt driveway.

He pulled into yet another drive blocked by a rusted and apparently locked gate. There was nothing on the other side of the gate except an empty plowed field, some neglected looking out-buildings and far beyond a line of trees, what appeared to be more empty camp spots. "No, I think the other gate was the right one. Let's go back." I urged, starting now to get stressed. It was still early in our trip. The thought of spending the night pulled over in the weeds by the side of the road was not an inviting one.

Steve backed the van out of the driveway, not an easy task with a manual steering, non-automatic-transmission vehicle. Shifting into reverse was a test of physical strength. He turned around in the narrow road and drove back to, and then right past, the first drive-way we had tried.

"Let's just go back down the road a ways." He said, repeating my suggestion as though it was his original idea. "I thought I saw some buildings back that way." Strangely, he sounded humorless. Was this an adventure, or an ordeal?

I bit my tongue and tried to quiet my loudly beating heart. I was experiencing fear, stress and frustration. Steve drove about a quarter of a mile to the next dirt driveway and turned in. It too was blocked by a neglected looking gate that appeared to be locked. From the light of the van headlights in the now deepening dusk, we could see a house or office structure, more out-buildings and what looked like some bungalows, but still no people and no lights.

"We were better off at the first driveway. At least there was a building there with lights on." I urged. This was getting uncomfortable. We were in the middle of what I considered nowhere, with no place to stay and it was now dark. We had made a pact before starting on the trip not to drive past sunset. It just wasn't safe to be out on the road when you had no idea where you were or where you were going.

Meeting Pipsqueak and La Dueña

Obviously annoyed, Steve backed out and turned around yet again, and headed back to the first driveway we had tried. Our headlights now shone through the gate and, as luck would have it, onto a man walking toward us.

"*Hola!*" called Steve. "*¿Tiene espacio?*" Asking if they had space seemed ludicrous. There was not another camper or vehicle to be seen in the camping resort.

"*Sí, sí.*" Replied Arturo, the gate keeper and night guard, as he unlatched the not-really-locked gate and swung it open for us to enter.

After a broken conversation in our bad Spanish and the gateman's questioning responses (*"¿Como?"* which is Spanish for "Huh?") we communicated that we needed a space to camp in for the night and would like to use the restrooms while we were here.

We learned that we were about three weeks too early for the "season." They had all the room in the world. In fact, we were the only guests in a huge camping and cabin resort surrounding a lake of the same name, *Cascabela*.

Like many things in Mexico, the resort appeared to have been built 20-25 year ago, then "let go" ever since. The huge pool had a water spout to swim through and overlooked the lake. It featured a little floating trash, and ominous gray shadows on the cement bottom.

We parked so that our van lights shone onto the side of the restroom building. The restroom building advertised itself as available for "Ladies" and "Gentlemen". About every fourth letter of each sign was missing. It seemed to read " 'adies" and " 'en leme", which could have been confusing. Especially since it was in English instead of Spanish. It should have read *"Mujeres"* and *"Hombres"* or as the neglected letters might have read " *'ujer s"* and *"Hom es.* I began to understand a whole new way of looking at the California gang culture's name for its members: Homes!

The water heater which was not connected to any faucet we could find was perched on a cement shelf, on the outside of the building, right in the front, partially obscuring the "men" in "Gentlemen." We tried to understand the plan behind this placement of the water heater. No pipes ran into or out of the tank. It was a tease, indicating that yes, we have hot showers here. We were soon to discover that this resort, with a promise of hot showers, was typical of many places in Mexico and beyond. We took a hot shower for granted north of the border. If your hotel had no hot water, the manager would hear about it immediately. Here, we felt lucky to have water at all. In fact, this particular bathroom had no water, no shower and no lights. It did however, have plenty of bugs.

We learned to appreciate little things. We were new to Mexico so expected such conveniences as water that works all night, not just until 7PM, or 11PM, or whenever the pump or *"La Bomba"* gets turned off. We came to appreciate the ability to actually flush paper down the john. This is just not done in Mexico. Instead, you place the used paper in a waste basket in the stall, if you can find a waste basket in the stall. It will be immediately obvious if it's missing, a pile of used tissues in the corner takes its place. This is usually a gathering place for flies and other insects and gives the area a distinctive aroma. This was the bathroom I faced, flashlight in hand, dead tired and

Meeting Pipsqueak and La Dueña

disheartened, early into our one-year-trip into Latin America.

Conveniences like lights, water, toilet seats and waste baskets aside, we were warmly welcomed and made to feel at home by three camp dogs, one of which Steve named Pipsqueak. Pronounce that with a Spanish accent, please. *Peepsqueeek.*

A Chihuahua-mutt mix, she was the smallest of the three dogs. Her run featured a little hop, performed simultaneously by both back legs, about every third step. You got the impression she was somehow skipping.

She had huge liquid brown eyes. Her tan face remained impassive and motionless, except for two brown eyebrows which moved up and down expressively when you spoke to her. Her eyes followed you everywhere, never missing a movement.

If you looked as though you were even thinking of a walk, she was up and ready to go, body alert, legs ready to begin their hoppity-skip. Were you tired? She instantly relaxed next to you, turned tummy-side up, just in case you felt the urge to scratch, *por favor.*

And when you closed up camp for the evening, she was on guard, resting on a little hummock of grass, ready to sound the alarm if anything should venture too near. And ever present was the thump, thump of an eager-to-please tail, making you feel somehow loved in this place far from home.

Later that evening, we met the other guardian of the camp, *La Dueña*, the boss. *La Dueña* was a diminutive little lady from Brazil. Size was obviously of no consequence, for she clearly struck terror in the hearts of her employees. Marleen was about 50, or 60, or who knows? She had bleached blond hair, skin as white as fresh milk and lips outlined in brown lip pencil. She cut a dramatic figure in this out of the way place.

We talked of many things during our evening visit including the glory days of the resort. Then it was truly a zoological refuge.

It sheltered deer, Canadian Geese and birds of innumerable kinds, and her favorite, iguanas.

Six or eight iguanas currently lived in the back garden near the reception area. What a shock to see a 6-foot iguana marching across the shaggy grass, munching on crickets, butterflies, beetles and whatever else was unfortunate enough to be in the way. One big orange and brown fellow sat on a cement wall, motionless for 30 minutes, then it snapped up an unsuspecting moth that must have mistaken him for a scraggly, misshapen tree branch.

La Dueña became highly emotional, even agitated at one point in our conversation. "Imagine!" She said in her perfect Spanish. "One guest brought two *"pistolas"* to our park! For what purpose, in such a place? Here everything is beautiful! And when he saw my iguanas, he shot two of them! Bang! Bang! Dead!" Her hands, shaping themselves like two guns, fire once, twice and drop to her sides in limp sadness at this statement. "My heart was sick! My spirit was outraged!" She raged now just thinking of the incident.

Meeting Pipsqueak and La Dueña

"Out you go! I told him!" She waved her hands forcefully toward the now locked gates. "No one is welcome in this place that could kill such beautiful creature!"

She was filled with emotion, just remembering the great loss of the two colorful iguanas. Her tone made me very glad I was nowhere nearby when the deaths occurred. How the sparks must have flown between *La Dueña* and the *pistola-*packing guest.

A woman of great courage, *La Dueña* told us of a trip she made alone by truck from Brasilia, Brazil to Las Vegas, Nevada. To make such a trip at all takes determination. To make it alone takes a superwoman. She gave us a copy of her itinerary, detailing the cities, mileage, time and money spent along the way.

The most amazing and unbelievable section of the route passed between Esmarelda/Posto, Columbia and Las Palmas, Panama. This part is unbelievable for one reason, there is no road. This section known as the Darien Gap is about a 100 mile lapse in the Pan American Highway. It passes, or fails to pass, through equatorial jungle and guerilla infested territory. And we're not talking about the furry kind of gorillas found in Africa, but the gun-toting kind found on the verges of civilization. We had found no book, map or internet site that detailed this section of road as passable in any sense of the word, or as existing in any kind of reality. Yet there it was in her travel journal, a trip taken in August of 1999.

"How can this be true, *Dueña?*" I asked innocently, so as not to offend or cast doubt on her credibility.

"It is possible." She replied with an air of certainty. "You must remember three things. Number one: Never be in a hurry or you will make a mistake while driving. Number two: Never pass a big truck if you are driving alone, especially at night. Number three: Not everyone is your friend."

And with a curt nod of her blond head and a pat on my arm, the discussion of long road trips through uncharted territories, and perhaps through life itself, was over.

Waking up in a lake!

> *"Let a smile be your umbrella, because you're going to get soaked anyway."*
>
> Unknown

Chapter 3

Waking up in a lake!

Just when you think you've found the quintessential Mexican paradise, you wake up in a lake.

Twenty-six miles of really nice, paved road brought us from the toll road just south of *Los Mochis* to Mr. Morro's RV Resort. It sat right on miles of uninterrupted beach at *Playas Las Glorias*.

We were welcomed by the classic Mexican color scheme: bright orange, sea blue and lemon yellow, all on the same building. We overlooked the potholes filled with water from yesterday's rain and the dirt paved "boulevard" leading to the resort, and pulled into one of the 80 RV parking spots. 77other spots stood empty. We shared the resort with a 5th wheel and 2 motor homes pulling extra cars. As usual, we were the smallest and oldest vehicle in the park. But who's keeping track?

Carlos, our host, was born in Mexico, but educated in the United States. He welcomed us with charming English to a palm-thatched, *palapa*-style dining pavilion. The waves crashed onto the nearby beach and the moonlight was reflected off the tile-lined swimming pool. Only the *"picaduras"* or small biting insects that joined us for dinner spoiled the ambiance.

Since we hadn't stopped for lunch, we dove into the all-you-can-eat seafood platter for two. For $21 US we had smoked marlin, 2 kinds of shrimp, one of which was stuffed with cheese and wrapped in bacon, and a whole fried fish and two or three different kinds of deep fried fish, the names of which are unpronounceable for us. Dinner included salad and a pitcher of fresh limeade, which we enjoyed despite warnings against eating local produce and enjoying drinks made from unfiltered water.

So let's see, good food, reasonable prices, on the beach, quaint, quiet, what else could complete this paradise? A light show, of course. The lightning flashed for 3 or 4 hours, giving us a show that you just don't see in California. It flashed horizontally and vertically, from cloud to cloud, and just generally lit the sky from horizon to horizon. Whamo! The noise of the thunder was continuous.

I am not sure when I fell asleep, but there was another surprise in the morning. Rain had fallen steadily during the night. The Mexican paradise was now in the middle of a lake. It surrounded the resort, covered the lawn, the parking areas, the driveway, and the road. Everything was 4 to 6 inches deep in water. This seemed like a very negative situation to us, but seemed normal to the resort employees. It must happen all the time, or at least every time they have

Waking up in a lake!

a heavy thunderstorm, or its winter, or high tide, or some other non-dry type of situation occurs. We were soon to learn that things which in the States might require engineering, drainage, restructuring or repair, here in Mexico were just *"normal"* and the thought of changing things that were "good enough" never even occurred to the residents.

"Gracias a Dios" for my high school Spanish. I was able to get an employee to guide all the camp guests through the water, over a gravel road and onto the good paved road that was above the flood level.

Slowly we followed the lead vehicle through the flooded parking lot and onto the boulevard. The water was up to and over curb height. We couldn't help but remember that this boulevard had been dirt paved and dotted with huge pot holes. Our guiding line was the center planting area which divided the lanes. It barely showed above the water level. We could plunge into one of the pot holes or high-side on the center divider. I glanced at Steve and noticed a fine film of perspiration covering his face and that his shirt was now soaked under the armpits. It just wasn't hot enough yet to generate this kind of physical response, so it must have been the thought of wrecking the van just a few days into our trip that threw him into a panic.

The other feature of the road that caused concern was the presence of deep ditches on either side of the road. Driving into one of these would plunge our VW into muddy, brackish water well past the bottom of our doors. It would flood everything inside. The idea of locating a tow truck here was inconceivable. If we had these kinds of thoughts while driving an old VW, think how anxious the owners of the new, expensive motor homes must have been as we inched our way along the flooded roads.

Our guide took us out the back way, through the local neighborhoods where women and small children watched from the glass-less windows of cement block houses. Water filled their yards and, in some cases, their homes. No one seemed all that concerned except for those of us in the caravan. We had options. We were on our way. These people lived with this kind of flooding as a matter of course. They had no options and weren't going anywhere. This small experience began to help us put our lives and opportunities into perspective. We had a vehicle and enough time and money to make a trip like this. Those watching us inch by through the flood waters did not. Any complaints that might have issued from our minds or hearts about the circumstances were stilled.

Mexico Map

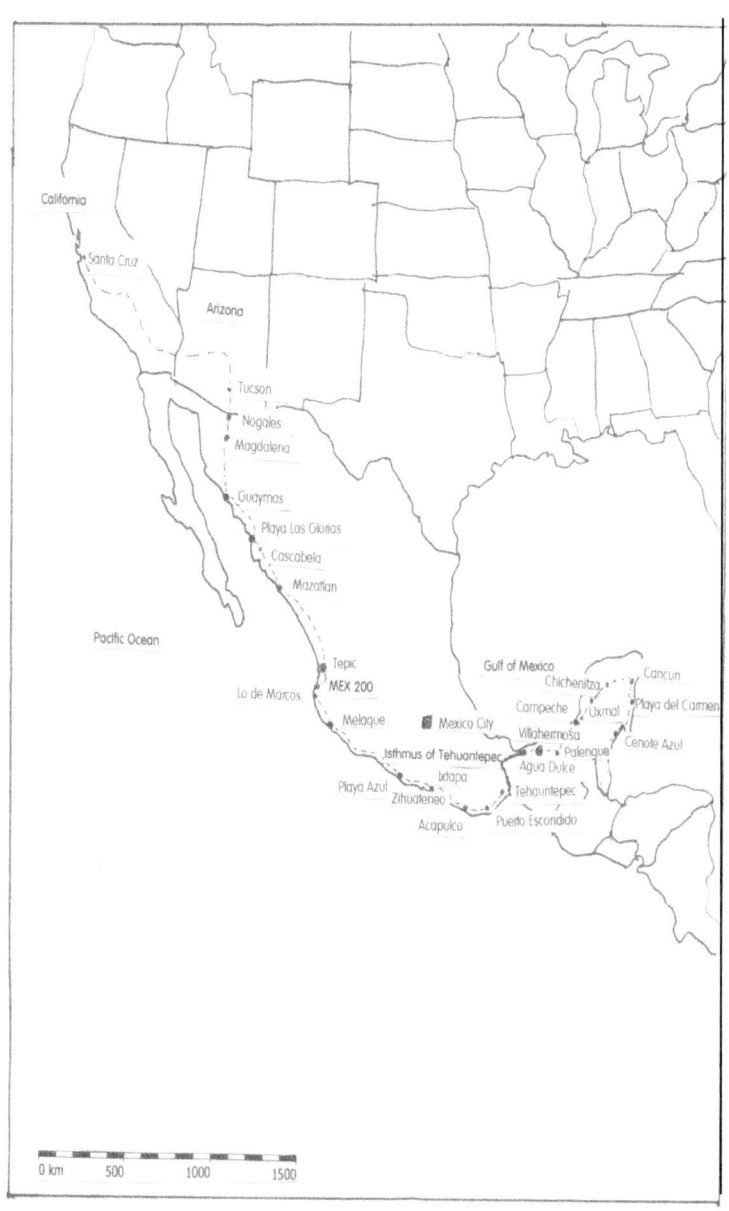

Mexico

"Truth is more of a stranger than fiction."
                                    Mark Twain

Chapter 4

The Attack of the Body Snatchers

A visitor feels so sought after in Mazatlan. The storekeepers want you. The street venders want you. Taxi drivers want you. Hotels *really* want you. The people are friendly because, of course, they want your business as a tourist. But you have a special importance to the Body Snatchers. You are their life blood, their reason for existing. Without you, they would starve, or at least have to find another line of work.

We were out for a walk on the first evening of our stay in Mazatlan. The evening air was as warm as a piece of soft cloth sliding across your skin. A breeze rustled the palm fronds. The mango margarita had just kicked in and life was good. Then we met the Body Snatchers.

Body Snatchers were really field representatives from the hotels and resorts in the area. Their job was to bring people in to their places of business. Once you were there, real salespeople tried to sell timeshares, condos or vacation packages.

That all seemed straight-forward enough. After all, everyone wanted to see the inside of some beautiful resort that was just up the beach from where you were currently staying. What were those places like inside? How did people afford to stay there anyway? We're all just naturally curious. The Body Snatchers were just providing a way to satisfy that curiosity.

Any problems caused by the Body Snatchers were due to competition. Competition is a good thing. It keeps prices in line, encourages innovation, and often creates real bargains for alert consumers. But among the Body Snatchers, competition had gone wild. At times they promised things that the resorts could not or would not fulfill unless you, the "body-snatchee", argued long and loud.

Incentives are a recognized way to encourage motivation for a sales person and stimulate purchases by consumers. Incentives in the Body Snatcher world took on a whole new meaning. The motivation to meet their daily quota of visitors was so high; they passed the incentives on directly to you. Would you visit a resort and listen to a sales presentation for two tickets to a dinner theater? How about for a cruise around the bay for your whole family? Not enough incentive for you? Let's try something everyone wants. Cash. Not *Pesos*. US Dollars! Is $40 US enough encouragement? Add a bottle of tequila, the real kind with a worm? How about $100 US, tickets for a show, a bottle of tequila, *and* a blanket to take home to where you might actually use a blanket. You won't need it here in paradise.

Attack of the Body Snatchers

The pursuit of your time was relentless. Name the price, they would try to accommodate you, just to get you to the resort site and meet their quota of so many bodies per day. And they were everywhere: in booths on the corners, leaning against walls, driving by in open cars, walking, standing, talking to groups of tourists. It was a Body Snatcher-filled nightmare.

Or was it? At first, we were annoyed. Every 10 feet someone called us *"¡Amigo!"* or asked "Where you from?" We got so tired of waving them off and saying no, that we changed our tactics and started bargaining with them instead. We learned they were real people, young men with families or just with ambitions. We learned about their "three-a-day" quotas, and their desires to move up to be a salesperson or a "closer."

We also learned about "playing the game". We were beginning to understand why some people consider life in Latin America to be *"la vida loca"*, the crazy life. There are some things that just don't make sense to a North American's way of thinking. The Body Snatcher's assignment was to bring in 3 or more live bodies each day, which was what they tried to do. The people they brought in might have absolutely no intention, or even the ability to buy. Who cares? They were breathing. They qualified. The object became to bring in the people, not to try to sell the timeshares. The cost of bringing in those people was very high.

Once you, as the consumer, learned how the game was played, the craziness meant that a Body Snatcher would outbid their competitors to get your time. Or even try to outbid their fellow salespeople at the same resort. Instead of them manipulating you to attend their presentation, you began to manipulate them by selling your time to the highest bidder.

You played the game; the Body Snatcher met his quota and got paid. You spent 2 or 3 hours visiting a beautiful resort and having breakfast or lunch with a sales person who treated you like you were one of the most interesting tourists currently visiting Mexico. Then you learned a couple dozen ways to say "No." and took your parting gifts and went home to your hotel. You might have made enough cash to pay for your hotel for two or three nights. You might go out for a dinner and a show on their vouchers, the Body Snatcher got paid, and no one seemed to care about the cost to the hotel or timeshare, even the people that worked there. Everyone was playing the numbers. Enough people bought to make the system work. And when we tallied up the bottom line for our week in Mazatlan, we came very close to costing Mazatlan money for us to stay there. Now that's crazy.

This was one way to look at Body Snatchers. We've heard horror stories, but every experience was either ordeal or adventure, depending on your attitude. You might run into a Body Snatcher on your trip to a resort in Mexico, and who knows, you might enjoy the encounter. We did.

> "Success is relative. It is what we can make of the mess we have made of things."
>
> T.S. Eliot

Chapter 5

A Hellish Night and the Morning After

It must have been the hand of fate that sent us to Tepic after we left Mazatlan. Fate, and the fact that it was the most direct way to access MEX200, a road which would crawl along the coast all the way to Acapulco.

At first it seemed fate had dealt us a difficult hand to play. Our van was repaired in Mazatlan after 4 days in the shop. Or was it repaired? Halfway through the four and a half hour journey to Tepic, we entered the mountains. The van had been running fine, then suddenly, the engine got noisy. Real noisy! We're talking backfiring, popping, and making big noises that make you think the engine will fall out onto the pavement at any moment.

We stopped along the roadside. Cars and trucks roared by, inches from our van. Drivers in Mexico are not known for their skill or consideration. We never did determine if there was actually a test that had to be passed to receive a driver's license. People we asked about this had differing responses. If there was such a test, many of the drivers that passed us that day had somehow missed the test and were driving without a license or the skills that it demanded. Once again, our stress levels were in the red zone.

Steve dragged out all the tools and checked the compression, hoses, sparkplugs, you name it. Everything checked out okay. Somehow that was not comforting. It would have been better if we had found something specific that was wrong. Not knowing why the van was running so poorly and was so noisy was unsettling. We had the feeling that we could be broken down again at any moment. We had no choice, so off we went. Except now the van would not start.

We were right back to where we had started before the time spent in Mazatlan to make repairs. Noisy engine, bad starter. We really had no options at this point. We were closer to Tepic than to Mazatlan. Steve crawled under the van, hit the starter with a wrench as I turned the key. It started and we limped forward, arriving in Tepic after dark.

One of the things you do not do in Mexico is drive at night. It is high on the list of no-no´s, somewhere between drinking tap water and eating unwashed fruit at roadside stand. But we were driving at night without options. There were no Motel 6's along the freeway here. We had to listen to the noisy engine and watch for big trucks with no tail lights, cows, burros, and goats *on* the road, bicyclists, and the *topes* or speed bumps that lurked at the entrance to every village that boasted more than one house. All of these things might actually occur at the same time. The needle on the stress meter had been hovering near the red before. Now it was in the zone and beyond. We were barely speaking to each other. Just driving in these conditions was

A Hellish Night and the Morning After

taking all our concentration. We had nothing left for conversation. If we had, it would have been in the form of an argument. Better that there was silence.

By this time we had opened every guide book and camping guide we owned. They all said something similar about finding your way around Tepic. Similar, but not exactly the same. The trick was finding the MEX200 turnoff that headed *into* town. Finding it in the dark was another story completely.

Now in the states, this would have been a no-brainer. See the sign, turn. But in Mexico it is a whole different game plan. First, you can't see the sign. They are not lit at night. They are not placed so that your car lights will always strike them and they are not reflective. They are not always placed so you can see them at all due to trees, brush, vines, graffiti, and worst of all, if you happen to be following a truck, the truck itself will hide them until it is too late to read them, let alone make the exit. The exit follows the signs *immediately*.

So up and down MEX15 we went, searching for the MEX200 exit. Finally we turned off the highway into the city and asked for directions at a couple of little shops.

You need to ask for directions more than once. It is considered impolite, a *"macho"* failure, to admit you are clueless about how to get somewhere. So any directions received are suspect. They may be completely wrong, partially wrong, or at best, confusing. But by processing three sets of directions, and throwing in the information from the guide books and a little intuition, you have a fighting chance of locating your destination.

Two If By Van

Karen McGinnis

We finally found the RV camp we were looking for. Now the cards we had been dealt were a little easier to play. The engine was still noisy and the starter still required the application of a screwdriver, but we were safe within a walled enclosure and had access to a toilet and shower. There was even a cross-eyed guard dog on duty.

Then we discovered the *real* reason why we had been "sent" to Tepic, and to that particular RV camp on that particular night. Fellow travelers that we had met on our first day in Mazatlan were one camp spot away. We had kept in touch by email and knew they really needed to see a friendly face. They had been sick and then wrecked their van. And all this had occurred in the worst possible place, Mexico City.

Now we learned the details of the illness (flu) and the accident (backed into a pole) and the extent of the damage to the van (crushed the back window and tailgate). Their personal nightmare grew worse as they had failed to find gas for their cook stove at the only dealer listed in Mexico. They were now traveling sick, broken and unable to cook.

They ran into the cultural problem of locals not wanting to tell a stranger "no" or "I don't know." They searched for solutions to their problems in one of the worlds most crowded and polluted cities and they had been sent on one wild goose chase after another. Finally, Alice had cracked, broken down in tears and swearing, and they retreated to the solitude of their van and made a dramatic decision. They were outta' there!

When we found them by chance in Tepic, they were heading for the United States as fast as they could. There they hoped to find solutions to their problems and a culture they could understand. We were familiar faces in a sea of strangers. We couldn't help, but we could listen and nod. After hearing their story, we shared our own problems. They almost felt lucky. Their back window was a piece of plywood held on with duct tape, their tail gate did not lock and they had no cooking fuel, but at least their van ran great.

Did I mention that these travelers were from Austria and that English was their second language and Spanish their third? They had started their trip in Alaska and were already half-way through their trip to South America.

Next morning, they headed for the border and Steve headed for our engine compartment. Again, everything checked out great, even the spark plugs. Where was the noise coming from? Finally, after leaving the engine running and listening carefully to every part of it, he spotted the problem. One too many bone jarring *topes* had broken loose the exhaust system between the catalytic converter and the muffler, leaving an inch-wide gap. The result of this gap was constant noise and backfiring.

We pulled into a muffler shop, got instant service, and drove out after having paid $15 US for welding and other services. Major improvement, the noise was gone. Then things got even better. Near the muffler shop was the exit ramp marked MEX200 heading toward the ocean. We felt as though a miracle had happened. We had spent hours the night before searching for this exact exit. Our nightmare in Tepic was over. We were on our way again on what would turn out to be one of the most beautiful routes we had yet to encounter in all of Mexico.

The Beautiful Road

*"With an eye made quiet by the power of harmony,
and the deep power of joy, we see into the life of things"*
                                                    Wordsworth

Chapter 6

The Beautiful Road

After a hellish evening and a productive morning in Tepic, we were rewarded for our perseverance with a drive along the most beautiful country road I had seen in Mexico.

Determined to stay on the road despite our mechanical annoyances with the 20-year old van, we set out on MEX200 which connected Tepic in the mountains with the coast, and ended up in the tourist Mecca of Puerto Vallarta.

This road was the perfect illustration of the concept that the journey, not the destination, was the object of travel. Leaving the congested mountain-top capital of Tepic behind us, we headed due west. The road wound through several mountain passes on the way to the sea.

The hillsides were covered with a veritable jungle of foliage. It started at the immediate roadside. There were no shoulders on the roads in Mexico. The road was bordered by grasses with feathery tops of the faintest shade of rose. Like tassels, they waved in the wind of each passing vehicle, enticing the passerby with their frothy fronds.

Two If By Van

Karen McGinnis

Interspersed among the rose-topped grasses were wildflowers in profusion. Spindly stalks supported brilliant orange daisy-like blossoms. Growing at their base were bright magenta blooms. And slightly further back from the roadside, the vines begin.

There were vines in the trees, on the rocks, the poles, the fences, the walls, the rooftops. Now I understood why the machete was the most valued object in a Mexican country home. It was the first line of defense against the vines. Some vines provided shocking purple morning-glory type blossoms. Their clinging vines and colorful blossoms softened things which without their colorful blessing would otherwise have been ugly, or at the very least, boring or ordinary.

On the larger trees, a yellow trumpet vine completed the landscape. Hundreds of bright yellow blossoms shouted with vibrant color. Competing for passing insects, they screamed with color in the already exuberant landscape. All this color was set against a backdrop of deep green trees, shrubs, palms and banana trees.

Suddenly we began to understand a little something different about Mexico. The countryside itself was not only colorful, it was brilliant. It shouted with life. It was no wonder that when it was time to paint their houses and shops, Mexicans chose bright yellow, purple, brilliant oranges, blues and other colors that reflected what they saw in nature all around them.

This flower-lined road wound through the hills then descended to rolling plains planted with sugar cane and mango orchards. The cane fields carpeted the valley and

The Beautiful Road

crept up into the hills. Like punctuation marks, the spiky fields of pineapple filled the spaces between the orchards and the cane fields. At the edges of the cultivated fields, the tree and vine-filled jungle waited for the chance to jump back into the open spaces.

Just when this amazing display seemed as though it would go on forever, the road dropped to sea level, and the shining waters of the Pacific stretched out beyond palm-lined beaches. We had finally encountered the Mexico of the tourist brochures, after almost a month of deserts, congested cities and car trouble. Here the beaches were wave-washed and lined with palm trees and *palapas*. Breezes were soft and cobblestones paved the village streets. The smell of sea food and fresh tortillas encouraged us to try the local fare. After weeks on the road, the beautiful MEX200 had finally brought us to the Mexico we came to see.

> "Men read maps better than women because only men can understand the concept of an inch equaling a hundred miles."
>
> Roseanne Barr

Chapter 7

What We Had Learned So Far

Our journey had brought us through many experiences. We now knew how each reacted when faced with off-the-chart stress. Steve descended into swearing and sweat-filled frustration. Lying on his back in dirt and stickers while trying to fix a cranky starter as trucks rumbled by just inches away, did nothing for his attitude. It pushed all his buttons at once. My attempts to be helpful which really did nothing to better the situation and were not taken as helpful just tipped the scales and plunged him into an abyss of nastiness. Everything I had ever experienced made me feel like somehow, this was "all my fault." What was that about, some possible recall of the fact that Steve had originally planned this trip as a solo adventure on a motorcycle? This hadn't been my dream trip. This wasn't my old VW van. I was mechanically challenged, so, by default, not responsible for repairs. Yet, there it was, guilt.

This pattern of interaction was not going to work. I looked ahead at months of stress and knew we needed to solve this action/reaction problem immediately. The only solution we could come to at that point was for Steve to ask me to take a walk out of ear-shot whenever he knew a swearing jag was imminent. While this did not fix the dysfunction, it did allow us to get through the stressful moments without destroying one another with words.

Steve may have had his moments with mechanical frustrations, but they paled in comparison to his reaction when he discovered that I could not read a map nor drive in Mexico. This even surprised me. While this was really something that was not really a fault, it was, under the circumstances surely an inadequacy.

"Where do we go at this intersection?" Steve would ask.

"I don't know." I would reply, while peering at a map filled with meaningless lines and symbols. I was helpless. I didn't even know where we were, let alone which way we should proceed from where-ever 'here' was.

"Can't you just look and see?" Steve would ask, as though I just wasn't trying.

"I am looking. Can't you see me looking? I just can't see where we are or where we are going or which way we're suppose to turn. I can't even see the intersections on the map!" My voice must have been breaking. I would begin to feel the tears welling up in my eyes.

"Do you want me to drive in this traffic and look at the map at the same time?" Steve would ask.

"No." I ventured, tearfully.

What We Had Learned So Far

"So can you drive while I look at the map?"

All I needed to do was look at the wild traffic that whizzed past us, remember the stiffness of the non-automatic steering and the manual transmission, and I knew that driving in Mexico was not going to be very successful for me. I had tried driving during our first days in the states and had been so stressed out and unsuccessful at it that I actually did no driving in Mexico and almost none in Central and South America.

Exasperated, Steve would pull off into a roadside turn-out and begin to read the map. If it is possible for vans to have body language, even the van was saying "Cheeze-louise, what a worthless travel companion you turned out to be." It didn't really help much that my middle name really was Louise! The truth was that this was exactly how I was feeling about myself at that time in the trip. After a few moments of studying the map, Steve knew where we were, what turn we should have taken, and how to get us back on the correct road.

This wasn't the first time nor would it be the last time that the twin challenges of map reading and driving would surface. Much like the swearing issue, we somehow worked out a solution. I did my best to read the maps, even tried to read them the night before, trace out the next day's route, and write down the names and numbers of all the turns we would have to make the next day. Mexico did not cooperate too well with this system. Often the roads were not labeled. Sometimes the map and the physical reality did not match. Sometimes I just missed the turns. We got good at turning around. Anyone who has ever taken a road trip knows what it means when you say "The tension was so

49

thick you could cut it with a knife." In fact, if a knife had been handy on several occasions.... Let's just say that Steve and I were both glad we were safely strapped into our seats and that the knives were hard to reach. While I tried my best to overcome my apparent map-dyslexia, Steve did his best not to come unglued when turns came and went and we obviously became lost.

It was a good thing we were safely back on the one road that ran along the coast. We needed a few days of downtime to de-stress after city driving, car repairing and hopeless map reading. During the next few days we found some quiet camping places near the water's edge. Sitting by the waves, reconnecting with each other, and using a flush toilet instead of a bush by the side of the road, really helped ease the strain of traveling. In fact, it was heaven.

> " 'Home' meant the house, but also everything that was in it and around it, as well as the people, and the sense of satisfaction and contentment that all these conveyed."
>
> Witold Rybczynski
> "Home, A Short History of an Idea"

Chapter 8

Home Away From Home

Just when I was starting to feel overwhelmed by all the tiny villages with dirt streets, just when the repetition of coconut milk vendors and *tortillaria* stands began losing its charm, just as small waves of homesickness started to lap at the shores of my emotions, at that very moment we pulled into Puerto Escondido and I was saved. Good-bye homesick blues, we were at a home away from home.

I had yet to see another town that shared so many characteristics of our own surf/tourist town of Santa Cruz, California as Puerto Escondido. It shared many features yet retained its Mexican charm.

The town itself ran unevenly along seaside hills and was split by a river that ran through it. Santa Cruz was laid out in much the same way. Neighborhoods furthest from the water catered to the immediate residents. There were small corner markets, auto repair shops, little hardware and clothing shops, and restaurants that fed those who lived near-by. This all felt so like home.

Close to the water we found hotels, small to mid-size, some with *cabañas* or cottages to rent right on the edge of the beach. In the center of the hotel and beach areas were the shops that catered to locals and tourists. T-shirt shops and shops with hand crafted clothes sat side by side. Local crafts and jewelry filled the shops, and were on display by vendors right at your feet, at curb level. Walk-around vendors brought the goods closer to your face, just in case you were too lazy to bend over to look at them. There were coffee shops, internet cafes, health food bars, and ice cream in every flavor known to, well, the Italians who owned the shop. Even the cheap souvenir shops made the place seem so familiar.

Talk about the food, every corner brought a taste of home. Fresh fruit smoothies called *liquados* graced every menu. There was seafood of every description, caught fresh and cleaned right on the beach less than a block away. There was pasta, pizza, vegan, stir fry, you name it. And of course everything came with a sidecar of rice and beans and a salad of local avocados and tomatoes. Were those washed before being served? Who cared?!

A nice deep breath really brought on a feeling of home. The deep rich aromas of street-side coffee shops, and pastry filled the air. The sound of local gossip and idle chit-chat invited this coffee-starved visitor to spend a little time healing a homesick heart.

The home town ambiance got even richer. Sitting there, sipping coffee, you noticed something else familiar: the people. The pedestrians-only street was filled with familiar faces. This was a surf Mecca, and the passersby's faces were ones you might see on the Pacific Garden Mall in Santa Cruz or the Capitola Esplanade or in any funky downtown coastal area. There were surfers with long hair, short hair, no hair, dread-locks, surf mops and vegetable dyes. They were dressed in board shorts, baggies, and saggies. They were accompanied by girls in bikinis, sarongs and every other style of dress and attitude you might see at home in the States.

These young Americans came to this relaxed and friendly town by bus, plane, car and thumb, although thumbing was the hardest way to travel in this spread-out country. They came for the surf, the sun, and the sand. The miles of beaches on this bay offered world-class surfing in no-wetsuit-required water. The locals even sponsored surf contests to attract the out-of-town talent.

Puerto Escondido, Mexico was a place that had a sense of itself. It spiced that sense up with a little salsa flavor, the savory smell of coffee, and when all was blended together, it cured my homesickness and inspired me to explore more of Mexico.

"We don't receive wisdom; we must discover it for ourselves after a journey that no one can take for us or spare us."
Marcel Proust

Chapter 9

Coast to Coast: Touching Mexico

At first I thought Mexico was a land of contrasts: the rich and the poor, the educated and the illiterate, the cities and the jungles, the deserts and the rainforests, the present and the past. After driving in a single day from the Pacific Coast, across the Isthmus of Tehuantepec to the Gulf of Mexico and into the cities on the Caribbean side, I came to realize it was something different. It was *all* of these things. Just like the elephant in the East Indian story that was described by the blind men, it all depended on where you touched it.

The north felt like endless deserts, filled with *saguaros*, organ pipe cactus, and *ocotillos*. The border state of Sonora was surprisingly green for desert and ran right up the sides of the Sierra Madre Mountain Range. The covering of *saguaros* on the mountain sides gave them a prickly look, like a craggy faced old man with a two-day beard. Touch Mexico here and you felt sharp edges, a harsh landscape and an environment that challenged its inhabitants.

Two If By Van

Karen McGinnis

Crossing into Sinaloa State it was as though God stopped there and planted a garden. Suddenly those same broad plains were filled with crops and orchards. The desert was blooming there, blessed by wide rivers and filled with irrigated, food producing flood plains. This part of Mexico felt gentle and hospitable to its caretakers.

Mexico a little further to the south created a whole new set of impressions. From Mazatlan to Huatulco, the coastal states of Nayarit, Colima, Jalisco, Michoacan, Guerrero and Oxaca offered Mexico with a tourist feel. Made-for-tourist towns like Acapulco and Ixtapa contrasted with unknown charmers like Lo de Marcos. This part of Mexico felt like sun kissed beaches, palms trees, the good life with a Big Sur-style scenery that inspired the imagination.

If you try to describe Mexico in terms of its big cities, your experience would continue to be varied and unusual. There was the traffic and the hustle-bustle of cosmopolitan life. There was culture, history, art, and education. It was packed into the cities. You also had to describe Mexico in terms of quiet cobblestone streets and walled courtyards surrounding lush private gardens. The variety continued in the cities as within blocks of the main thoroughfares were the down-and-dirty, gritty sides of congested urban life.

Crossing from the Pacific to the Gulf of Mexico by way of the Isthmus of Tehuantepec exposed flat, swampy stretches interspersed with hundreds of acres of farm land. This part of the country felt like relief from the mountains of central Mexico. Its flatness prepared you for the shock ahead.

The Gulf of Mexico was a shock. It was flat. No waves. The land of the state of Veracruz seemed to run right out into the water. The land level limestone shelves do exactly that, buffering the coast from waves and creating crystal clear turquoise water. It was easy to see how hurricanes that hit land here could do so much damage. Rising water of even a foot would swamp houses, restaurants and highways along the water's edge. Add a little wave action, and you'd have a disaster.

The states of Campeche, Yucatan and Quintana Roo were filled with jungle. So lush was the vegetation that it hid a 50 foot high pyramid that was just 30 yards away. Here Mexico felt cold and clammy in the cloud forests, hot and muggy in the jungle rainforests, and after hiking an hour off the main road, all your Indiana Jones dreams started to come true. The land felt old, the stones were old and mold covered, the buildings were older than could be imagined and hid secrets that were still being discovered.

Mexico was many things, and felt very different depending on where you touched it. Perhaps the best part of touching Mexico in so many places was how it touched you in return and left you forever changed.

"The man with a clear conscience probably has a poor memory."
Lawrence J. Peter
"The Peter Principle"

Chapter 10

Getting Peeped

After a typically hot and frustrating day of driving through unmarked roads and congested villages filled with unlicensed drivers, we began searching for our next camping spot. Our guidebooks told us that somewhere nearby there was a place to spend the night at a former sugar plantation. Since our dream for the future included moving to Maui, Hawaii, a place known for raising sugar cane, this seemed like an ideal place to get the flavor of the future. We were still expecting signs to direct us to the plantation, or at least a road-side marker with the name of the place or the street address. These were not in place, but we tried driveway after driveway within the range indicated by our guide books and eventually found the plantation.

Whoever described it as a "former plantation" was a master of understatement. It had not been a working plantation for so long that it resembled a cluster of ramshackle buildings and very little else. The "campground" description was also suspect as there were no other campers there and no official places for campers to pitch tents or pull up vehicles. It still looked good to us after a long day on the road.

We were welcomed by the wife of the "campground manager" and her three children. She directed us where to park near a thatch-roofed shed and showed us where the unlit and neglected bathrooms were located. She had a delightful smile, an easy laugh and barely came up to my shoulder. I felt extremely tall and thin. Her children watched us shyly. They were hesitant to speak to us until Steve pulled his stash of soap bubble toys out of the van. They were instantly fascinated. Adults and children alike had a wonderful time blowing bubbles, chasing bubbles and posing for pictures as we blew and chased bubbles. Apparently bubbles are part of a universal language.

Before night fell, Steve and I set up camp, which consisted of moving all the stored items off the bed, opening the back hatch to allow air to flow through the hot-box of a van, and attaching the mosquito netting to the now open back-end of the van. After spreading out the sleeping bags, sheets, and pillows, we showered and prepared a simple meal. As it grew dark, we turned on our battery powered lights and settled in to an on-going game of cribbage. The competition was intense. At the beginning of the trip, I never won a game. As time went by, my skills increased, and by the end of the trip, I was winning too much of the time. Steve had lost interest in playing by then and it was a challenge to generate a game.

As we were playing, I began to smell smoke from a cigarette. It would waft into the van. I looked out into the surrounding darkness, but saw nothing, no lights, and no people, just the sound of crickets and frogs in the night and

Getting Peeped

the rustling of the breeze in the palm thatch. The smell of the cigarette smoke became more constant. I began to feel as though we were being watched. Putting the two together, I told Steve that I was sure someone was watching us. Without changing our posture or stopping our game, we began to discuss just where someone could be watching us from and how we would confront them. Tucked away in a cabinet under the sink we had a high-powered, rechargeable 5-million candle-watt spot light. Initially we had thought this might be handy if we ever needed to make repairs at night, encountered wild animals in the jungle, or needed to find our way over rough, unpaved terrain in the dark.

Steve retrieved the spot light and in one smooth motion, slipped out of the van and shone the light on a spot under the low hanging thatch of the shed behind us. There, hidden among the fronds was the "night watchman/security guard" for the campground. It must have been a slow night for him as he had chosen to "watch" us very closely. Hidden in the fronds, with his white shirt off to make himself blend into the darkness, he had been observing us. Confronted by Steve and blasted with the spotlight, he reluctantly came forward and offered a multitude of conflicting reasons why he was lurking there, within feet of our van, in the dark, partly clothed and silent. It was obvious to us that he had been "peeping" us, hoping to see something of interest. Surely *"turistas"* did things differently, they must be worth watching.

While Steve and my Spanish ran the gamut from university-classroom to street-smart-functional, it was adequate enough to give him a good tongue lashing for invading our privacy. He appeared shocked that we were able to speak to him in his native language at all, and understood his lame excuses as being inadequate explanation for lurking in the shadows. Caught by the spot light, he seemed unable to make his escape until Steve turned off the light and bade him *"Vaya!"*

While the incident left me shaken and somewhat insecure, it did reinforce our routine of not undressing where we could be watched. This stood us in good stead later when we joined a group of Canadians parked behind a hotel. The showers and bathrooms were on the lower level, under the main building, backed up into the hillside. The ventilation for the showers opened to the crawl space beneath the building. We learned from our fellow campers that workers from the hotel had a habit of crawling into this space and watching through the ventilation screens as the camping guests showered. While I showered in my bathing suit, I could not help but wonder what the draw was that would make crawling through the dirt, encountering scorpions, centipedes and bugs of unknown types worth the potential show.

> *"The closest anyone ever comes to perfection is on a job application form."*
>   Unknown

Chapter 11

Learning About "Good Enough"

The concept of "good enough" was pretty foreign to me before I spent time in Mexico. Oh, I admit, I had tried it on for size a few times, especially when dealing with meaningless, repetitious tasks. On the whole, "Do your best, or don't do it at all." was a lesson my father taught me well. I learned a whole new way of thinking in Mexico.

Some people think Mexico is the land of *"mañana"* or tomorrow. I disagree. "Good enough" was more realistic. *Mañana* indicates that there is an intention to do something in the future. "Good enough" clearly tells you that what you see is all you are going to get. It will be exactly the same way *mañana*.

In day to day living, "good enough" worked like this. The toilet has no seat, but it still flushes, right? OK, that's "good enough." No need to replace the missing seat. The door to your room couldn't be pulled closed and latched because the bottom was warped, but it didn't swing open by itself either. That's "good enough."
The extension cord that brought power to the washing machine ran through standing water on the floor, draped

over the hot and cold faucets at the kitchen sink, was spliced with masking tape, then plugged into a splitter before being plugged into an ungrounded socket. No one had been shocked yet, and the machine ran. It's "good enough."

The nice new tile that lined the floor and walls of the bathroom was a few tiles short here and there, so another color filled in the empty spaces, where ever they might have occurred. The electrician couldn't come to set the electrical boxes in the same room, so just break out a hole in the new tile with a hammer, put in the box later, then fill the broken spaces with cement. The room was still waterproof and now the lights worked. It's "good enough."

There was no road sign warning of a bone-jarring *tope* (speed bump) that sent all your possessions, including your head, crashing forward like projectiles. There was a rock set on the side of the road to keep you from going around the bump at the last moment. That's "good enough."

There were hundreds, maybe thousands of other things that were "good enough." Some I wasn't exposed to. Some I became used to and didn't notice after a while. Most of the "good enoughs" were the result of circumstances beyond people's control Materials, money, or craftsmen just weren't available when needed. Some "good enoughs" represented situations where the current state was so much better than what previously existed that they really were "good enough."

In some instances, "good enough" represented the best that could be achieved or that could be expected. I had learned that so far we were alive, healthy, clean, fed, rested, washed, and generally in great shape. Despite minor inconveniences that were "good enough", which were really just variations from perfection; we were having a wonderful experience in a beautiful country.

"Chamberlain's Law: Everything tastes more or less like chicken."
--from The Official Rules

Chapter 12

The Colors of Belize

As we entered Belize, I expected to see a country that was a cross between Pirates of the Caribbean, Bob Marley's hometown, and a village from the seacoast of England. This sovereign, English-speaking country was the size of Massachusetts with a population similar to the entire County of Santa Cruz, California. I expected it to be sparsely populated and very rural. It had been the home port of choice for English pirates, and its logging industry had been worked by slaves imported from West Africa. The resulting mix of cultures was not exactly what I expected. It was diverse and colorful, but clearly a reality and not a fantasy.

Immediately after crossing the border with Mexico, the road in Belize became wider with a nice, mowed, grassy shoulder. This was especially welcome as we had become used to roads with no shoulder at all while driving in Mexico, where at best the side of the road was bordered with deep ditches filled with murky water. Mexican drivers came at you unexpectedly at breakneck speed. Several times a day, assuming death was imminent, I said my prayers, certain that a head-on crash with a careening truck filled with melons would be a part of my obituary.

Here in Belize, swampy, lush jungles continued on both sides of the road just beyond the neatly mowed shoulder. Houses became more substantial, with just a few stick, mud and thatch houses appearing here and there. Here houses had doors and windows covered with shutters, the perfect adjustment to the muggy, hurricane prone climate.

The bright colors of Mexico mellowed under the tropical sun of Belize. Here a soft gold or white was the normal paint color for houses. As we drove deeper into the country, we saw more houses and trim painted turquoise to match the color of the Caribbean Ocean and shades of purple to compliment the flowers. The biggest change of all was the addition of wood siding and Victorian style trim. After months of seeing houses made of sticks, handmade adobe, cement block and exposed rebar, this architecture and color seemed charming.

Belize radio broadcasts were a mix of Barry White, Motown, blues, Christmas carols, gospel and jumpin' reggae. Everyone seemed happy in their own colorful and slightly eccentric way. Creoles and Garifunas, a mix of races from the original settlers, added to the ethnic mix of Central American Indians and African descendants. Throw in East Indians and Chinese and you have some idea of the racial and cultural makeup of Belize. Life in Belize was many things, sometimes poor, always colorful, but never boring or homogeneous.

We approached Belize City through lowland jungles filled with standing water and swamps. Houses stood on amazing

The Colors of Belize

8-to-10-foot tall stilts, or sat slumped in the boggy ground. Because the land was so flat and so often swamped by hurricanes and torrential rains, the ground was permanently saturated with water.

Belize City itself was neither Disneyland nor an English Village, but a collection of wood-sided houses, aging and neglected. They sat crowded together on extremely narrow streets that were bordered with open gutters on each side. Even here in the city, standing water was an issue. A careless misstep sent you calf-deep in water that had been standing so long, it had fish living in it. These weren't really gutters, they were streams. Below the streets in the States one found storm drains which handled this water. Here in Belize, below the streets was more soggy ground. There was nowhere for the water to drain off, so it stood in gutters and low places, a welcome home to mosquitoes, small fish and a watering spot for rats and other small mammals that made the city their home.

We had heard that you were more likely to see a jaguar than street signs in Belize. This turned out to be true. While we never saw a jaguar, we also never saw street signs. Addresses on store fronts helped, if you had time to stop and read them without the bustling traffic running up your back bumper. City traffic moved at a frantic pace. Many streets were one way. Unexpected u-turns took place constantly. Once again, our stress meters were bopping in and out of the red zone as we tried to navigate our way through narrow streets, bordered by deep gutters filled with water while facing traffic patterns that bore no resemblance to anything we had encountered so far.

In the countryside, if faced with an unmarked intersection of two roads, friendly locals waved you in the right direction for tourists, or pointed in the opposite direction from the one you were headed. They intuitively knew where you were going, toward the next tourist attraction or park. We often had no idea we were lost or going the wrong way, but the locals knew, and were cheerfully willing to redirect us. This local helpfulness lightened the mood as Steve struggled to turn the sluggish van around on narrow dirt roads without backing up into a water-filled ditch or sinking axle deep into soggy ground.

In the small towns, signs without directional arrows indicated one-way streets but had cars parked in both directions. Trying to figure out which way was really the "one-way" was nothing more than a guessing game. We just plowed ahead. If we got stopped, at least we spoke the right language, English, to ask for help. Hopefully the police would take pity on the stupid tourists who had such poor driving skills that they had gotten themselves into yet another mess.

There were no camping places within the city limits of Belize City. The best we could hope for was to be allowed to park in the driveway or yard of a guest house. After navigating the sign-less streets, we finally located one of the guesthouses listed in our guide book. There was just barely enough room to pull our van off the street and into the driveway. A gate closed behind us, providing some protection from the bustle of the street. Despite this precaution, at some time, perhaps when the gate was open, the black plastic caps that covered the air valves on our tires were stolen. We had just spent months in Mexico, camping in some very unusual places and nothing had ever been taken from our van. We had been here in Belize just a few hours and already we were being pilfered.

We had a suspicion that is hadn't been someone off the street, but one of the guest house children who had taken the caps. We were in a sticky situation. Making a fuss over what might seem like worthless pieces of black plastic could put us out on the street with no place to stay for the night. That would not be a good thing. I was all for just blowing this off and ignoring the missing parts. Somewhere in Steve's soul lay a sense of right and wrong that could just not let this go, and he knew that checking air pressure in the tires from then on would be a problem. After much discussion, he decided to bring the issue up with the hostess of the guest house.

Try to picture this situation. Steve, who obviously did not need to work while traveling for a year in a vehicle that looked like something upscale here in Belize, was complaining about losing the plastic fittings to his air valves. In the hostess's mind, Steve was now accusing her son of stealing. All this was taking place while we were parked in the driveway of her run-down, single-walled house that probably would have been bulldozed if it had been in the United States. Something about this confrontation seemed out of balance. Miracle of miracles, even though the hostess adamantly refused to believe that her eight year old son could have possibly taken the caps; they appeared on our cooler the next morning. We didn't ask any questions or even mention them again.

We took a walk through Belize City in search of some local food. Our guide books referred to the Royal Rat as a delicacy of the area. We were on a hunt for a restaurant that catered to local folks and served this treat. We strolled through the streets, hopping over the water-filled gutters and noticing the rats that darted in and out of the drains. We met some interesting local characters. One dreadlocked gentleman wobbled in our direction and in a mixture of English, Creole and drunken slur, asked if we were interested in purchasing some hash. Now Steve loves hash, but the corned beef variety. This was not what the local was offering. After thanking him politely, and making a hasty retreat, we kept a wary eye out for other vendors of illegal substances that might think we were the opportunity for a quick sale.

Luckily we happened on a restaurant/bar that featured rat on the menu. We ducked inside and were ushered to their best table. It was up a narrow flight of stairs and located on a narrow veranda overlooking the city. The evening view was spectacular. The rat arrived in a sort of stew that camouflaged its true nature. Steve fulfilled yet another culinary goal. He added rat to the long list of weird creatures that he had eaten in strange places around the world. I had something tame like fish or pasta. Can you guess which of us is the more adventurous?

"To travel is to discover that everyone is wrong about other countries."
Aldous Huxley

Chapter 13

On the Water in Belize

Belize's major attractions were its cays or keys, off shore reefs. We visited Caulker Cay. A water taxi speed boat with twin outboard engines zipped us across the crystal turquoise water. At speeds of 30-40 mph, the trip through the reefs and ever-changing shades of water was exhilarating. Submerged cays and reefs were marked only by sticks that stuck up out of the water and were secured in the unseen coral. The unusual color of the water was mesmerizing. It varied between bright turquoise, deep turquoise and a blue-green turquoise, depending on the depth of the water. The shoreline was ringed with bright white sand. Here and there along the shore we saw a mansion with its own dock, or a shack with its own rickety catwalk built of salvaged lumber and sticks. Rich and poor shared this paradise.

The charming, sunlit cay welcomed us with bright colored buildings and shining white beaches. The sand was so white because it was made up of ground coral and tiny shells. Sand streets were lined with small bungalow hotels, restaurants, email cafes, and houses built on stilts.

Everything was neatly spaced for plenty of breathing room. The space also allowed the waves to wash over the island during tropical storms and hurricanes without taking down everything in their path.

Because the white beaches were really collections of tiny shells and bits of coral, they were sharp on the feet. Water shoes were a must as we waded out into the warm water, dropped face down, and snorkeled out to view the conch shells, coral, sea grasses, fish and other wonders of the tropical sea. The water was bath temperature. Conch shells the size of a man's head lay on the sandy bottom. Conch was a local favorite and was served in restaurants as appetizers, main courses, and if they could figure out how to fix it, as desserts. It was plentiful and easy to obtain. Depending on where you bought the food, it was either cheap or expensive. I guess some places just saw the tourists coming.

We reluctantly left the tropical cays behind and water-taxied back to Belize City. Clouds piled up on the horizon and we ran a race with the coming storm. We continued our road trip through the Cayo District of Belize where pasture land and upland forests were filled with rubber trees and *quanacaste* trees, butterflies and spider monkeys. Steve played Tarzan on the hanging vines and we spent a few lazy days at a tranquil camp spot in this lush countryside. Our hosts had all our needs covered. They had a restaurant, bar, art gallery, email center, gift shop and tourist guide service. All this was located within steps of our campground and their house. They even found a VW mechanic to fix our valve problems. The soft warm evenings were filled with fireflies dancing on the grass, blinking their messages to one another in the fading glow of the sunset.

On the Water in Belize

Belize didn't meet my unrealistic expectations. It exceeded them with its friendly people, unique landscapes, and its naturally brilliant colors. I'll just have to visit Disneyland or go to the movies if I want to see the Pirates of the Caribbean.

> "Nobody, as long as he moves about among the chaotic currents of life, is without trouble."
>
> Carl Jung

Chapter 14

The Border Game

Steve negotiated his way through the dirt-paved parking lot. Staring us in the face was yet another frustrating and disorganized border crossing. Several mismatched buildings sported signs saying Customs, Immigration, Department of Ecology, *Turismo*, etc. There was no indication which we should visit first. Is it Door Number One, Door Number Two, or.....?

Just when you pick one, and open your van door, your border-redeemers arrived. Non-official locals appeared from nowhere. For a small fee, they would gladly guide you through the customs maze, help you play the border game, change your money, and generally make your life easy once again. All this was included in the price of a small tip and the agony of having them "in your face" the entire time.

Steve, being a man of vast experience at border crossings around the world, chose to go it alone. My choice was to stay in the van and protect it and all our possessions. This usually was accomplished by rolling up the windows to avoid all the players in the border crossing game. Steve was left to run the gauntlet alone. The first window he approached was set in the wall at the level of the average American stomach. For Steve to talk to the agent inside required bending over, then holding that undignified pose throughout the whole process. One window, one fee down, how many more to go?

The next window would only take Guatemalan *Quetzales*, so directions were given to the bank. An indirect wave of the hand in the general direction of the village and a "on the corner" in Spanish sent Steve trudging off down the street and across the bridge to some unknown corner, somewhere in the village.

A semi-alert customs agent realized that the *gringo* was headed into the next country without his proper passes, stamps and fees and took off running to catch up with Steve. In their combined English, Spanish and Spanglish, they eventually understood each other. Steve was personally led to the bank, on the corner of the customs building itself. Ooops!!

Window Number Three required a fee for the car, and a signed statement that we would not enter Guatemala and sell the car. Now that's a novel idea, drive 4,000 miles, cross the border and sell the car you consider your sanctuary and salvation. Then what? Cheerfully walk to *Tierra Del Fuego*? No problem, we signed the paper.

The last and final window (are we big winners yet?) required a fee for the parks and ecology of Guatemala. Now that's a worthy cause, but no free passes to enter the parks? We could consider it a parting gift?

The Shores of Lake Yaxha

Relieved just to be on our way, we passed the guard at the turnpike, crossed the bridge, and stopped at the turnpike on the other side. There yet another guard requested yet another fee for the "city" we were about to enter. It went to maintain the streets (dirt) and the law enforcement (him?).

Then they sprayed our van for any bugs that might be hitchhiking across the border on our bumpers or wheels, and we paid yet another fee. Drained, confused, poorer, and not feeling much like winners in the border game, we entered Guatemala. The jungles, lakes and volcanoes of Guatemala lay before us. We had successfully passed through yet another gauntlet on our journey to the end of the road, *Tierra Del Fuego.*

> "Life is either a daring adventure or nothing. Security does not exist in nature, nor do the children of men as a whole experience it. Avoiding danger is no safer in the long run than exposure."
>
> Helen Keller

Chapter 15

The Shores of Lake *Yaxha*

We rolled onto a fairly decent black-topped road after we entered Guatemala. There were a few rock and water filled potholes. We had driven over worse in our trusty van. Unfortunately, it was the wrong road.

Friendly locals chuckled a little and pointed toward a gravel road that led into the jungle. Were they laughing because it was the "right road" and we just couldn't tell due to the unmarked intersection? Or was it yet another "wrong road" that led to nowhere? Since we were already in the middle of nowhere, we might as well go all the way there.

After about five miles of gravel and washboard road, we humbled ourselves yet again and asked a local woman walking along the road with a tray of vegetables on her head if she knew the way. She again chuckled slightly, and informed us we only had about 15 more miles to the "real road". Did that mean this wasn't a real road? So many questions, so few answers, such bad Spanish.

The bumpy road rolled on through jungles of trees, vines and swamps. Here and there stick houses and small pastures broke through the dense growth. Wiser men than we rode horses along the side of the road. Then, just as the woman had predicted, the road turned "real." The wide, asphalt-paved passage through the jungle had cement gutters on each side and was clearly marked with road signs. We were entering the part of Peten, Guatemala where tourists pass on their way to the Mayan ruins of Tikal.

Our immediate goal was Lake *Yaxha* and the third largest Mayan ruins in Guatemala. Open less than four years, the site was relatively unknown. Years later, when we were happily living on Maui, we would see a season of "Survivor" that was shot in this very park. We reached the guard station for the site at 5:08 PM. Closing time was 5:00 PM. Dusk was falling. The nearest city or campsite, other than this park, was hours away. The guard took pity on us and raised the gate.

Steve put his master-driver's hat on, and negotiated the next three miles of rutted, washed-out and rock strewn dirt road in the near dark. Then after one particularly steep downhill stretch, we burst into a meadow right at the lake's edge. The setting sun had left a pink glow on the mountaintops and across the water of the lake. The blue and violet water was like glass. The reflection of the mountains was crystal clear.

The Shores of Lake Yaxha

The camp was, of course, empty except for one group of backpackers settled into a thatched cabaña. We chose a grassy spot right at the edge of the lake.

Night fell. The moon shone full and bright on the still water. Bats dipped and darted through the night sky. Doves bobbed across the grass, cooing and searching for fireflies that flickered off and on in an erratic ballet. Then, through the tranquil stillness, came the sounds of motorcycles downshifting on a steep grade. No, make that loons calling to one another in their characteristically raucous voices.

Daybreak came early and abruptly. Howler monkeys screamed at one another in the surrounding jungle. Screeching like jaguars, they scared the uninitiated and made those wise to the sounds of the jungle sit up from a deep sleep and bonk their heads on the ceilings of camper vans.

The brightening sky revealed dense jungle all around. Steep hillsides rose from the water's edge. A stairway cut into the hillside climbed from the camp area straight up, pausing at an information area, then continuing into the plazas of the ruins. After about 50 steps, your calves hurt. After about a hundred, they ached. Somewhere between 100 and 200, they started screaming. Blindly, focusing on each foot fall, we worked our way up to the flattened areas on the hilltop.

Seven partially restored plaza areas greeted us. This lost city covered the top of the mountain, commanding sweeping views of the lake on one side and the seemingly endless jungle on the other. In the distance, the howler monkeys kept up their verbal reminder that this was all "for real."

After visiting each partially restored plaza, climbing several partially restored pyramids and feeling the immensity of the city that had once flourished here, we turned back toward the lake.

A cut through the jungle led to the lakeside. Spider monkeys thrashed in the treetops on the sides of the trail. Swinging from tree to tree, they grabbed fruit, husked it and after popping the tender flesh into their mouths, sent the empty husk crashing to the forest floor below. There below the canopy, the sun dappled the vines and litter of leaves. Brilliant blue, and black, and red butterflies danced through the shafts of light.

Sitting still on a fallen tree near the path, the environment dominated our every sense. The sights, the sounds, the odors of the ripening fruit, even the feel of the insects from the fallen tree filled that moment with life. We were consumed by the fullness of the jungle.

The reality of the jungle was very intense. It became even more intense when we reached the lake. There, on a hand-painted sign was a warning against swimming in the cool water. Below it was a crude drawing of an alligator. It is a jungle out there!

"Honey, you were smelling bad enough to gag a dog on a gut wagon."
The Ballad of Cable Hogue (1970)

Chapter 16

A Garret in Guatemala

Steve and I had often joked about returning to graduate school and becoming starving students once again. In the Guatemalan village of San Andreas, we had a chance to try the experience on for size. We enrolled in a week-long Spanish class, 4 hours a day for 5 days. To enhance that experience, we lived with a local family during the week.

The school seemed pretty basic, one large room filled with tables, chairs and whiteboards. The windows looked out on Lake *Petan Itza*. The director of the school rode with us through the steep cobbled streets to the house of our host family.

There was a mother, father, two adult daughters, a teenage daughter and an eight year-old boy in the family. It was not immediately clear if the two adult daughters lived there or lived elsewhere. Our Spanish was okay, by this time, but it was entirely possible that what they were telling us was what they wanted us to know. Things were just not clear. Sometimes you just did not ask questions. By local standards, this was a very rich family in this town of 6,000 people. They had an inside bathroom and a two-story house made of cement block, which stood on a knoll overlooking the village and the lake. They had furniture and a yard and a vehicle. After seeing houses made of hand-shaped adobe brick and sticks stuck into the earth, we knew enough to know what local affluence looked like. The husband had a job as a *"jefe"* or foreman at a factory. This made him a person of some importance.

We were led up outside stairs to a huge attic room, a garret by definition, with a large dormer window and a lake view. There was also a small closet-like toilet facility in this space. We knew enough to recognize this as luxury. None of the surfaces in this room were finished. The wood was raw and the ceiling was sheet rocked but not taped, textured or painted. There was no insulation, so the glass-less windows provided not only a view of the lake, but also a cooling breeze in this hot-box of an attic.

I had an uneasy feeling from the moment we walked into the room. Steve sensed it and asked the director of the school and the hostess to excuse us for a moment.

"What's up?" He asked, convinced something was wrong. Women hate hearing that question. I could never quite give a satisfactory answer. I wasn't sure what was wrong. It was just a feeling.

"I don't really know. Something just isn't right here." I replied.

"Well, compared to where we might be staying, this seems pretty good. I say we take it."

We took the room.

Later that evening, I discovered what had instinctively given me such an uneasy feeling. We settled in for the evening and began studying our Spanish papers. We began to sense we were not alone. A slight rustle in the corner, the sound of small feet above the ceiling, scratchy sounds near the window, our attic garret was infested with mice. There weren't just one or two mice. There were dozens of mice. This space must have been empty most of the time, so the mice considered it a safe place to live and raise their families. We found after some exploring in the yard at the bottom of the stairs just why there were so many healthy mice in this house. Almost directly below the stairs was a chicken coop. Inside was a small flock of chickens. The feed for the chickens was placed in a shallow pan. Chickens being what they are, they liked to scratch and jump in their feed. The result was that the feed was scattered all over the ground. It was perfect for mice.

When we went to do our laundry in the washroom off the back of the house, we discovered an additional food source for the mice. The dog food was in a bag on the floor of the laundry which was an open air shed. The dog food was scattered all over the dirt floor of the laundry. No one ever swept the room, so the mice considered this a dining room as well as a place to get water and escape any cats that might be harassing them. Food was abundant, and hiding places were available. It was a mouse heaven.

Determined not to over-react, we turned out the lights and lay down on the too soft mattress. Sleep did not come for me, although Steve dropped off in about 30 seconds. As I lay listening to the sounds of life in the walls and ceiling around me, I happened to glance out the open dormer window. There, silhouetted against the window trim in the moonlight was a small visitor. The tiny mouse hung onto the center divider of the window and peered into the room through the open window.

I hit him with my only weapon, a flashlight beam. He scampered off, just as some relative of his dashed through the 4-inch gap under the door. I closed the window shutters, but could do nothing about the door gap. The restless night grew even longer as the frustrated mouse at the window spent hours scratching and chewing to get in. This was, after all, his home and we were only temporary visitors.

Day dawned with no mice in sight. A black scorpion crawled across the ceiling and disappeared into a crack in the sheetrock. Aughhhh! It had been safer in the jungles of Lake *Yaxha*. Attic garrets were supposed to be quiet, romantic places that created memories to be cherished for a lifetime, not places where you fought the wild life for bed space and lived to experience sleep deprivation.

That night, determined not to give up our space to the critters, we closed and locked the shutters early, blocked the door gap with the too-soft mattress, and placed sleeping bags on the box springs. Then we discovered the importance of the door gap. The un-vented toilet facility soon filled the room with sewer gasses. The smell was over-powering. We were now trying to sleep in a room that stunk, was probably bad for our health, and had occupants that might sting you or bite you or at least run over you as you lay sleeping.

This was the last straw for me. I bailed and escaped to the safety of the van. Steve stuck it out, popped in ear plugs against the mouse noises and prayed no one would light a match in the room during the night.

Neither of us slept much that week. We were pretty grumpy, bleary-eyed Spanish students. The teachers assumed this was our normal state of being. The week passed, verbs were conjugated and mice were shoved off the bed as Steve valiantly fought to maintain superiority in the gas-filled room.

Our experiment at returning to school received mixed reviews. The class was a success. Living like starving students in an attic room can only be described as an experiment in sleep deprivation and animal control.

> *"The rain follows after the forest."*
> The Little Book of Aloha
> By Renata Provenzano

Chapter 17

On the *Rio Dulce*

Traveling due south from our school site at *San Andreas*, we arrived at the inland port of *Rio Dulce*, Guatemala. The cramped little town sat at a narrow spot on *Lago Izabal*. This inland waterway was once the only access to the interior of Guatemala from the Caribbean.

Pirates made it an exciting place to live. They fought over it constantly. Now it was a bustling scrabble of street-side vendors and shops. It held back the jungle with its backside and welcomed ocean-going craft to its front-door marinas. It was to one of these marinas that we went looking for a place to camp.

The first marina we visited had a few modern day pirates. They sat in the bar at mid-day, hunkered over cups of coffee or bottles of beer, avoiding the direct light of the tropical sun. They might have been called wharf rats in any port city in the world. We beat a hasty retreat. Despite the fact that this spot was on the water, had a restaurant and a decent bathroom, the denizens weighed in more heavily than the advantages. We consulted our guidebooks and located another place to put down our anchor, or our ice chest and chairs, in landlubber talk.

On the far bank of the *Rio Dulce* sat a jungle hacienda and marina. The road to it wound around the port and snaked its way through grasslands, swampy areas and hills. The road itself was just rocks and dirt. Huge ruts that surely would have captured our van were filled in with tree branches to keep vehicles from disappearing into the muddy water that filled the indentations. This all made for slow going, and where we were going was not really all that clear anyway.

"Are you sure this is the right way?" I whined, sure that by now we should have seen some sign of the resort we were searching for.

"You've got the guide book. What does it say?" Steve replied. We were reliving yet again the exchange that repeated itself almost daily during this trip. He knew very well that I had no tolerance for reading while driving, let alone while driving over branch-filled ruts on dirt roads in the middle of nowhere. Beside that, we had had to ask permission to even drive on this "road" from the gate-keepers who lived in a small house near the main road. They had told us that the resort was "just up the road" which might mean anything. We had come to know that this might mean blocks or miles away. You just kept driving until you either found it, or gave up.

The guide book was worthless. The brief description didn't even match the road we were on. I had no confidence in following directions of a writer who obviously had never even passed this way before writing the summary. It did mention that the resort could be reached by boat. Since we had a vehicle and not a boat, the option of access by boat was out. Perhaps the writer had arrived by boat and completely bypassed this road of mud and ruts.

Then we got to the fun part of the journey to the *hacienda*. We had arrived at a parking area at the dead end of the road. We would have to leave our van here, parked with two or three other cars in the dirt parking area in the middle of a cow pasture. A wooden walkway led into the swampy jungle. It became a swinging bridge anchored to posts sunk into the muddy ground. The half mile of suspended plank walkways bounced and swung as you walked over them. Now I knew why the Boy Scouts called them "monkey bridges." You clung to the rope supports along the sides with every appendage you had, just like a monkey.

Since it had rained that day, the boards were wet and scattered leaves provided extra slipping opportunities. The suspended walkway paused at wooden platforms, and then continued over murky, debris-filled water. With a little imagination, every submerged log looked like, well, a submerged log. It wouldn't be until later in the trip that I discovered that what sometimes looked like a submerged log was really an alligator, crocodile or caiman. We pressed on through the jungle, over the swamp and through the trees. Steve even took my picture, hanging on to the rope handrails for dear life. No wonder my son back home had begun to refer to me in his emails as NGM, National Geographic Mom.

Our reward for a successful crossing of the swamp was a thatched marina, free of wharf rats, inhabited by backpackers and yachters. The French owners had 500 acres of swamp, pastures, river and lakefront property, waterfalls and natural swimming pools. We enjoyed a lunch, spent some time chatting with the other guests and relaxed after an anxious walk on the wild side of the Guatemalan jungle.

We quickly made friends with some of the other guests and arranged to spend the next day exploring the lake, the *Rio Dulce* and the Caribbean seaport town of Livingston. All would be accessed by a hired launch. Two sales representatives pitched their tours to us, each one touting theirs as the best available. Both would go by boat across the lake, up the river, stop for lunch, spend some time sightseeing, and then return us to this same spot.

Splitting the fee five ways made it very affordable. We would share the trip with Phil, a white-water rafting instructor for Outward Bound in Costa Rica, formerly an engineer in New Jersey. Betty was a computer systems designer from San Diego, taking a year off to see Latin America. Else was from Holland on a two week vacation. She worked at a bio-diversity museum, tending tropical vegetation in a glass enclosed environment. As a solar contractor and teacher, Steve and I rounded out the assembly of travelers. It was a great group to share a river trip.

We had to pass back through the jungle to reach our van, and then drive back over the rutted road to the gate house. With the marina owner's permission, we camped there in the yard by the gatekeeper's house. Of course it rained during the night. The ground around the gatekeeper's house was covered in lush grass. Once wet, the grass was as slick as snot. Our tires spun and we went nowhere. Steve had planned ahead for just such a situation. We had brought along boards to put under our wheels. Unfortunately, they were in the very bottom of our roof top Thule box. To reach them, we had to unload everything else that was in the storage box. It was drizzling, so the process of taking everything out was not a dry one. We did our best, covering things that might get wet or damaged. Fortunately almost everything in the storage box was already encased in plastic bags to guard against road dust.

With the help of the boards, we managed to slip and slide our way back onto the road. We repacked everything, including the now muddy boards, and off we went. Today's passage over the rutted road was even more exciting that the trip the day before. Today we had the added element of rain-slick mud. My life continually flashed before my eyes whenever I felt our tires loose their grip and the vehicle begin to go sideways on the road. It was a tense journey.

The early morning weather was "iffy" and threatening more rain. The launch we were to ride in had no sidewalls but did have a roof, so we took the chance. One of Steve's favorite sayings is "Take care, take a chance." This means, don't do anything stupid or life threatening, but do something. We were now going to live that saying. The launch engine required a few cranky attempts to start it, but eventually the pilot was successful and we were off.

The bridge at the *Rio Dulce* rose in a sharp wishbone shape. The height allowed sailing ships and freighters to pass freely beneath it. Driving across it was a real treat for cars. Its steel and concrete surfaces stood in sharp contrast to the dense vegetation on either bank.

Heading east under the bridge toward the Caribbean, we passed marinas and mansions where yachts and sailboats were moored. Between them sat the homes of indigenous people, sitting either directly on the muddy ground or built on stilts. Their canoes were hand carved from local trees and sat so low in the water that when returning from a day of fishing, there was barely any freeboard. The contrast between houses and lifestyles along the river was dramatic. Paradise continued to be shared by rich and poor alike.

The jungle embraced the river. The mangrove trees sent feelers down into the water. There in the tangle, the life of the river and the life of the forest intermingled. Fish found a habitat. Forest creatures caught the fish. The oxygen and nutrients exchanged promoted the shared health of all.

Snow white egrets and white and gray herons, coots and loons filled the water, skies and trees. Pelicans dove for fish, and then flew off, looking prehistoric against the clouded sky.

Around the *Isle de Flores*, the water lilies brought the jungle greenery out onto the water once again. There, floating in the sun, the lilies burst into gigantic white and yellow flowers. Birds walked across their buoyant surfaces.

Further up the river, white limestone cliffs provided sheer sides to the river passage. Waterfalls dropped hundreds of feet into the water below. We stopped at the base of one cliff where hot sulfur water bubbled from the rocks. The water was too hot to sit in without the cooling river water nearby. You soon forgot the distinctive egg smell in the joy of the warm water.

On the Rio Dulce

Our next stop was a *biotope* preserve where we walked along a rainforest trail...in the rain. The vegetation was diverse and reminiscent of a tropical plant nursery gone wild. Everything was gigantic and vibrantly green. Plants you might see in a doctor's office waiting room grew here to be as big as rooms. We all maneuvered carefully along the wet, rocky trail. It was only later, after our hike that we lost our footing on the leaf covered cement at the visitor's center. Onc by one we slipped and fell flat on our butts.

Else was in her element in the preserve. As a tropical plant specialist, she knew the names and characteristics of many of the plants we saw. Her joy at seeing these specimens first hand in their native habitat was palpable. Despite the gray day and drizzling rain, she was radiant.

We had lunch during a downpour in Livingston. Thankfully we had umbrellas as it was a torrential rain that soaked the unprotected to the skin. Many locals paid no attention to the rain, and just walked on as if nothing unusual was happening. Perhaps it wasn't unusual to them, this being the tropics. The water was not life threatening. We sat in an open air restaurant, watching and listening to the rain through the glass-less windows. The Garifuna town of Livingston was on the Caribbean Ocean. No roads reached it. It was linked to the rest of Guatemala only by its ocean and river traffic. It took very little imagination to picture pirates and seamen hiking up the steep streets, looking for a good time after months at sea.

The trip back to the resort hacienda on the river was fast and furious. Our tour was over. No point in wasting time on sightseeing now. The pilot put the pedal to the metal and flew through the rain. The jungle slipped by in a blur.

The rain stung our faces. We held tight to rain jackets and plastic bags and tried to stay dry. We felt very alive.

All too soon we were back at *Rio Dulce*. From our companions we had learned about white water rafting while sitting in hot sulfur water, about plant protection while hiking through rain soaked vegetation, and about the beauty of Guatemala while flying through the wet world of the river. The trip on the *Rio Dulce* was a sweet experience.

"Push on—keep moving."
                              Thomas Morton (1797)

Chapter 18

The Start of the *Ruta Maya*

Mexico, Guatemala and Honduras were studded with dramatic Mayan Ruins. The paths between the ruins that had been traveled by the Mayans were called the *Ruta Maya*. Our exploration of the ruins had actually started with Tikal in Guatemala the previous year. Unsure about whether we could successfully travel in Latin America, we "tried it on for size," taking a short trip and returning to the safety of the United States to discuss the adventure and plan for the future. Could we handle the traveling, the delays, the canceled flights, the broken down shuttle buses, the heat, the humidity, the bugs, our lack of Spanish skills...and still enjoy the experience? The answer was yes.

The previous year in April, when we had only been thinking about this van trip, I had one week of Easter Break in my teaching schedule. Steve was already in Guatemala taking Spanish language lessons in *Antigua*. His trip had been mostly paid for by a medical trial through John's Hopkins University. He played the role of a guinea pig. The idea behind the trial was to see if the medication they were

Two If By Van   Karen McGinnis

testing would 1) prevent you from getting travel sickness, otherwise known as "the two step", Montezuma's revenge, or diarrhea, or 2) help you to have a mild case of the same, or 3) none of the above, as they would just give you a placebo that did nothing. You did not know what to expect.

For all this uncertainty, they paid you enough to fly there and back and stay for the four weeks it took for the drug trials to run their course. In Steve's case, option 3 occurred. He had diarrhea the whole time. Either the drug did not work or it actually gave him the symptoms or he was receiving the placebo. To this day, he has no idea what actually happened. While there he stayed with a Guatemalan family, occupying a room the size of a closet that had the vague aroma of mold. Given Steve's allergies, the reaction to the room coupled with the travel sickness must have made the four-week trip agony.

In true Steve-style, he honked his nose, rushed to the john, and persevered. He conjugated verbs, named nouns and visited the local watering holes with his instructors and classmates. In the process he learned street-Spanish. I arrived three weeks after class started. He had planned well. We would have a nice room at a hotel, tickets for flights to Tikal, and he would meet me at the airport and escort me to *Antigua*. Here is where his plan broke down. My flight arrived a little early and because of that I sailed through customs. I was only bringing a carry-on backpack for the week and had nothing to declare. It took the customs agent a matter of minutes to figure out I was not a threat to national safety, and not aggressive enough to be smuggling anything. He waved me through.

The Start of the Ruta Maya

I walked through the airport terminal, noticing that it was two stories tall with restaurants and tables lining the upper balcony. I reached the front door of the airport and saw just beyond the door my first glimpse of life in Latin America. Immediately beyond the door were policemen in uniform. Beyond them were army trucks and men in military uniforms. Next were taxi cabs and drivers of all descriptions, all in uniforms and all vying for the traveler's attention. Crammed around the exit doors were family, friends, and tour operators, all pushing and shoving, trying to meet family members or attract business. I soon discovered that once I passed through those doors and exited the airport, the quiet and safety of the building would be lost to me. I would be adrift in that scrambling, roiling mass of uniforms, men and voices.

After checking the inside of the airport again for Steve, I exited into the melee. I was immediately thrown into the midst of men and cat calls and solicitations in a humid tropical world. Where was Steve? He was nowhere to be seen. I backed up against the glass walls of the building and surveyed the chaos. Surely he was here somewhere in this swirling mass of humanity. I had just spoken to him the day before. He seemed excited about my arrival, promising surprises. Well, so far this was a surprise alright. I began to try to figure out just what I would do if he had been delayed or worse, lost somewhere between *Antigua* and the airport. I did not have his phone number in *Antigua* nor the address of the family he was staying with. I was pretty much alone and on my own.

Do you know that feeling when your throat starts to tighten up and your eyes get really hot? I knew that I must be sticking out like a sore thumb in this scene, the only 5' 10" blond woman with a backpack. I was obviously attracting lots of attention from the policemen, the military men, and the taxi drivers. I fought to become as inconspicuous as possible. Bursting into tears at this point would not help me go un-noticed. I just wasn't ready to be on my own in a foreign country. I had not mentally prepared myself for this possibility.

Just then, I glanced at the stairway that led down from the restaurant level. There, large as life and about 10 pounds lighter than when he left home, was Steve. He looked as though he hadn't a care in the world. He had finished the pizza lunch he had been eating when I was passing through the airport. I could have killed him on the spot. He saw me waving frantically at him and burst into a wide grin. He didn't know that the tears I was crying weren't just from joy at seeing him. They were also tears of relief at being rescued from the unknown.

Our walk through the neighborhoods around the airport on the way to our home-stay began to enlighten me to the true nature of life in Central America. Streets were roughly paved and full of potholes. Traffic flew by and pedestrians were fair game. Curbs and sidewalks were broken, uneven and littered with trash and broken glass. Weeds were the landscaping of choice and high walls were topped with broken glass to keep us out and them in. The air was smoky from burning trash and cooking fires and the sky was a gray color I would learn represented smog in its rankest form. Here and there bursts of color peeked over high walls in the form of bougainvillea flowers and front doors and shutters were painted in hues that would make decorators around the world cry out in agony. What had I gotten myself in to?

The Start of the Ruta Maya

At the home-stay near the airport, we were shown a tiny room with a soft lumpy bed and all the mosquitoes you could handle, all included with the bland breakfast of hard rolls and over-ripe fruit. We had to yell over the wall to the host when we came back from a walk to get dinner because the gate was locked and the door bell did not work. The house did have a lovely back garden even if it was surrounded by a shard-topped wall. I learned that the political unrest that had existed for decades in Guatemala made the wall style a necessity to preserve the security of the family and possessions inside.

Steve had made arrangements for us to catch an early morning flight to Tikal. Of course the flight on the prop plane was overbooked. We did not have the sense to rush the plane and get the first seats. We had to wait in the sweltering heat for the plane to return from its first flight to Tikal in order to pick us up for a second trip. All this seemed so normal to the people in the flight company office. So the other plane was broken. No problem. Just sit. The plane we do have will be back for you. Now this worked out for us okay as we had a whole week to explore Tikal. Some of the other passengers were not so lucky. Some had only a day or two at the most. Waiting for two or three hours meant they missed their shuttle connections to the ruins and might only have an hour or two to explore before flying back to the city. They were not happy and the complaining became intense as we sat on overturned buckets and broken wooden boxes, waiting for the plane to return. Steve and several other men visited the office again and received assurances that the flight company would provide a shuttle for us from the airport to the ruins at Tikal.

The flight over the jungle was eye-opening. There below us rolled mile after mile of trackless jungle. Here and there a hut or two dotted the landscape. Fires burned everywhere. The pilot informed us that the fires were necessary to clear the jungle. I had not thought about this slash-and-burn type of jungle clearing before seeing it first hand from the plane. The burned landscape did not resemble the green jungle it replaced. Scraggly patches of crops struggled to survive in the newly cleared soil. They broiled under the tropical sun. Sporadically the farmer's children trudged back and forth from hand-pumped wells to water the crops. Clearly the system was inadequate to produce crops and did not justify burning such massive amounts of jungle. The fires created smoke-filled skies and a surreal appearance to the landscape below.

Once in the tiny Tikal airport, we waited none too patiently, as the airport personnel first told us we had missed the shuttle, and then scurried to round up another one when the crowd off the plane began to get boisterous in their disagreement with the possibility that they were stuck in the airport. Why would we all have flown here to the middle of nowhere to sit in an airport that had no taxis and was not within walking distance of anything? Shuttles were found, mutiny was averted and we all set off for Tikal.

The scenery we passed on our way to Tikal was dismal. The struggling farms looked even more desperate from ground level. Windowless schools with no desks or chairs or blackboards sheltered hordes of children and one teacher who was desperately trying to maintain order. How she taught anything to this conglomeration of children was unknown. I could not help but think of my own private school classroom, filled with materials and resources, and the rows of seated, controlled children. Did those children in America know how lucky they were to be in that school instead of this dusty, featureless room in Guatemala? I knew that I felt lucky to be teaching there and not here.

Halfway to Tikal, our shuttle bus broke down. We were now stranded on the side of the road, without food and only about a half a bottle of water for eight people, and no idea how we were going to reach our destination or be rescued from our plight. After sweating in the sun for about an hour, the bus that had taken the other half of the passengers to the ruins approached on its return trip to the airport. We flagged it down, although our driver seemed unconcerned and did little to assist us. The working bus loaded up our bags and our bodies and off we went. We left the other driver behind, and for all we knew, he spent the night there by the side of the road, in the middle of the burned out jungles near Tikal.

Tikal delighted us with its massive pyramids set deep in the jungle. No shuttle buses drove to the site, so it was hike in or don't go. The 50-to-60 foot high structures barely peeked out over the top of the tree canopy. The un-restored pyramids and residences hid under mounds of strangler figs, philodendrons, vines, leaves and debris. The surrounding jungle delighted us with free-flying green parrots, screaming howler monkeys and mischievous spider monkeys who tried to drop...well, stuff, on us from the trees above the trails.

Tikal was a wonderful introduction to the Mayan culture. The surprising size of the pyramids inspired Steve and I to research the *Ruta Maya* and plan ahead for our up coming visits to more ruins as we traveled through Mexico and Central America.

How did these magnificent structures come to be here in the middle of the jungle where now only peasants lived to scratch out a meager living from the poor thin soil? Was there more water then? Was the soil richer? What had changed in the agricultural patterns that made growing food possible then and nearly impossible now? What happened to these people who had built 50-foot pyramids, leveled the jungle, installed drainage systems, water catchments, market places, housing and recreation areas and lived a lifestyle that no longer even vaguely resembled the lives of current residents? We would ask ourselves these questions again and again as we traveled among the ruins of the *Ruta Maya*.

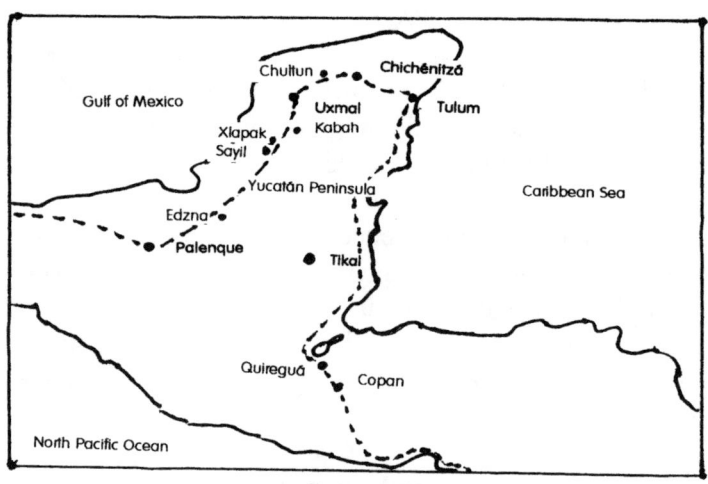

The Ruta Maya
The Mayan Civilization encompassed the Yucatán Peninsula in present day Mexico, Guatemala, Honduras and El Salvador.

"Tomorrow is the most important thing in life. Comes into us at midnight very clean. It's perfect when it arrives and it puts itself in our hands. It hopes we've learned something from yesterday."
John Wayne

Chapter 19

The End of the *Ruta Maya*

On our extended van trip through Mexico we visited *Palenque*, *Chichen Itza* and *Uxmal*. These were among the best restored sites. All had well developed museums, visitor centers and light-and-sound shows. The size of the structures and the amount of jungle that the ancient Mayans had cleared to accommodate the cities was overwhelming.

Smaller, less developed and more intimate ruins made exploration more personal. *Kabah*, *Sayil*, *Xlapak* and *Edzna* each offered different types of decoration, construction and lifestyles.

At a tiny roadside ruin called *Chultun*, Steve had a chance to get "up close and personal." Each site had a resident caretaker-guide. The attendant at Chultun was so happy to have someone, anyone, stop at the tiny site that he personally spent over an hour showing Steve around.

Born nearby, the attendant's father was a ranch owner. He had studied archeology at the University in Mexico. His slow and careful Spanish made the details he shared about the site understandable and enlightening. He talked about the ceremonial purposes behind each structure. He showed Steve how piles of "rocks" at most archeological sites were really storage places of hidden treasures. He turned over some stones lying in the grass. On the other side were carvings and glyphs, hidden from the world, waiting for the money and interest that would reveal their secret meanings.

I couldn't help but notice as they walked from structure to structure that there was a striking difference between the two men. One was tall, slender, and fair skinned with green eyes. The other was short, stocky, and dark and had eyes like deep, ancient pools of dark water. The buildings were clearly built to accommodate men of short stature. The low arched doorways made Steve look uncomfortable as he bent to enter each one. The guide walked straight through with ease, at home in this ancient environment.

After the building tour, they walked along the roadside, and then turned to examine a 1000-plus-year-old well. It was built by the Mayans and still provided water today. Like so many things that we saw on the *Ruta Maya*, this well was a practical link between the ancient past and the modern age that existed in rural areas.

The Mayan puzzle of the Olmec heads in the *Villahermosa* Museum sat in a replicated jungle setting. Exactly how the heads were made and transported was unclear. The giant rock heads made you think of other giant rock heads, like the ones on Easter Island. Was there a link between these ancient sculptures? Signs in the museum put one theory to rest. They stated, "These ancient civilizations did not have help from extraterrestrials."

The End of the Ruta Maya

They seemed very sure of this. The observer still wondered about the dispersal of similar sculptures throughout the ancient world, the construction of huge structures without the use of metal tools or the wheel. The sudden loss of vitality in the huge centers of population and the dispersal of the people who never again used the technology also raised many unanswered questions.

Tulum was our last Mayan ruin in Mexico. The city was built overlooking the Caribbean. Their buildings are out of square and set on unbalanced foundations. The dramatic differences between this younger city and the ones that were built hundreds of years before it were obvious. The technology was fading; their attention to detail was no longer a priority. Did this signal some weakness in the civilization that ultimately led to its demise? Yet another puzzle of the Mayan world went unsolved.

Our last three sites on the *Ruta Maya* were *Yaxha* in Guatemala, *Quiriga* and *Copan* in Honduras. The spectacular museum at *Copan* offered a full size, full color reproduction of a temple found inside a larger, plainer pyramid. The original had been completely buried beneath the larger structure. The reproduction offered an appropriate closure to our exploration of the Mayan culture. Its surface was covered with intricate sculpture created from stone and plaster. The entire structure was painted in reds and blues with white accents. The carvings and relief work were dramatic and frightening with stylized mouths opening to the underworld, giant jaguars and monsters holding people in their grasp.

Surely the buildings built by the Mayans we had seen throughout Mexico, Guatemala and Honduras had inspired fear in the hearts of the common man. The fear had further inspired loyalty and servitude, sacrifice and dedication. At the height of these emotions, the culture had flourished and conquered. Then, when emotion died, the culture disappeared. Only the Mayan people themselves lived on as ill-fitting residents of the modern world.

> *"The mistakes are all there waiting to be made."*
> Chessmaster Savielly Grigorievitch Tartakower

Chapter 20

Safe Camping

The 23rd of December was spent in the parking lot behind the police station in Cedona, Honduras. It was the best place the sea-side village had to offer. We had originally planned on staying in a spot on the coast called *Punto Raton*. We should have known better. In English that means Rat Point! That small seaside village boasted a cantina and bait shop on the beach, and very little else. When we inquired about a place to stay, one of the local residents was all too happy to take us to see a *"muy bonita casita"* or a beautiful little house. He claimed he was the agent and authorized to rent it to us. After squeezing through a locked gate to get into the property and tramping through a yard filled with downed palm fronds and weeds, we were not so sure. Once inside, the *"bonita casita"* was obviously abandoned and filled with dust and mouse droppings from the front door to the back. As politely as we could, we made a hasty retreat and thanked him profusely for trying to swindle us and rent a house that was obviously not available for rent.

Our next stop was Cedona. Here, a slightly larger and more complex cluster of buildings surrounded the beach and fishing pier. The streets were dirt, but this was Honduras, we had come to accept that amenity. We stopped at the one hotel on the main street. We were shown the "one available room" by the owner's son, a young man of questionable intent. The room looked to be one step above a brothel, with a lock on the door that had obviously been kicked in fairly recently. The only bath for the hotel was down stairs and featured a dark cement tub in which you stood while someone (?) poured water over your head for a shower. Not only did they want you to pay for this room, but they also advised you not to park your van on the street, much too dangerous. This was sounding better and better...sign me up! They offered to park our van at their house, just a few blocks away. That did not comfort me. After the encounter at Rat Point, this all smacked of something unsavory.

When in doubt, go to the local police station. This was just down the street. After meeting the police chief and his deputy, sharing our personal story, and the fact that my son was a police officer in the United States, we became fast friends. We took the chief and his deputy out to dinner. He invited us to camp in the weed and dirt parking lot behind the police station. He would even let us use the latrine and bucket shower at the station. Now this was more like it. As a bonus, we were able to run an extension cord from the station to our van so we could have lights and a fan to cool the van after a blistering day in the sun.

Feeling safe, we used the facilities and settled in to sleep. Morning came before we knew it and then we received our biggest surprise yet. There, across the dirt lot, about 20 feet away, was a small square cement block jail building. The two door openings were somewhat blocked by wooden pallets cut to fit the openings. There inside one of the doors, with his arms hanging out from between the slats was an inmate. He had been incarcerated during the night and we hadn't even heard it. He had been involved in a bar fight the night before and had been arrested for attacking someone with a machete. Now he was our neighbor. The pallet door to his cell was just a pretense. We had thought we were safe at the police station, but instead may have exposed ourselves to the one violent offender in the whole town. I was hoping for something better for the 24th and 25th of December!

A Different Story

> "My religion consists of a humble admiration of the illimitable superior spirit who reveals himself in the slight details we are able to perceive with our frail and feeble mind."
>
> Albert Einstein

Chapter 21

A Different Story

On a recommendation from the owner of a local auto parts store, we found *Hacienda Guiliaguime* in *Choluteca*. The *hacienda* had large rooms, hot showers, a pool and a restaurant. We enjoyed the chance to wash off a little road dust, use a real toilet and sleep in a real bed. It was amazing how far we had come in our appreciation of the little things.

We had agreed not to exchange gifts. We'd already given each other the gift of time and a chance to take a trip together that we would always remember. Besides, we knew that people were more important than things, and we had each other.

We went for a walk as Christmas evening fell. From the bridge outside of town, we watched the sun set over the volcanic mountains in the distance. The sunset was a gift in itself, wrapped in red and gold and pink. We lingered until the colors faded, then started back to the hotel.

We noticed some severe damage to the bridge railings on the upstream side. The guard rails and girders were bent inward. Something large coming down the river had caused the damage. The question was how? The bridge was at least 30 feet above the river bed.
We discussed this at some length and still could not imagine how this damage had occurred. Surely water had not risen this high. It would have been up to the eaves of our hotel and over the tops of many of the adobe and cement block houses that lined the river banks.

As we entered the hotel grounds, we stopped to chat with the night guard.

"What caused the damage to the bridge? Did Hurricane Mitch in 1998 hit here?" We asked. We were unprepared for the answers.

Francisco was an older man, on the tall side, fit for his age, with thick salt and pepper hair, and glasses. He wore his guard's uniform proudly and with a certain flair. He pulled himself up to his full height. I had a feeling he was mentally preparing himself for what he was about to tell us. Here is his story:

"The hurricane hit and we were not prepared. No one warned us it would be so bad. You know this is a poor country. People do not read newspapers. Many people do not have electricity. They can't watch TV or hear a radio. We were not prepared for what would happen. It was nothing we could imagine. It was not something we had in our memory, our experience.

"People in the city knew more than we did. They have more. Many people here have nothing. After the hurricane, they had even less. Less than nothing. Many did not even have life.

"The rains came and did not stop. This was misery. People live in houses made of adobe and sticks. Their roofs leak. Their floors are damp and cold. With so much rain, they ran out of firewood. Without wood, you cannot cook food or heat the house. People were cold and wet. Children were crying. They were hungry and cold and wet. Parents could not comfort the children. Everyone was scared. We did not know what would happen.

"You know that many people go into the woods every day to gather wood. It was wet. The trails were wet. Wet like running mud. They could not gather wood. They went and they came home wet and sick and the wood was wet. It would not burn. They could not heat their homes. They were sick. They were cold. Women could not cook and children grew tired of eating the same cold food every day. No tortillas could be made without a fire. It was misery.

"Still it rained. All the streams filled with water. All the low spots filled with water. The paths and trails and meadows filled with water. In the mountains, the rain washed down the gullies. It took the roads with it. Then it started taking houses too. You have seen the small houses of sticks?" He watched our faces intently to be sure we were following. He knew what was coming.

"Whoosh!" He said, both hands sweeping from high above his head to down below his knees in an arc. "Down go the houses. And the mothers and children are still inside.

Many, many people died, washed away by the mud and the water and the rain. Many people were already sick. They had no strength to fight the water. They just died.

"Right here," He pointed toward the nearby riverbank. "We found a mother caught in a tree. She had her baby wrapped in a shawl and tied around her." He motioned around his body in an X with an imagined baby held tight against the mother's chest.

"We were too late. The mother was dead. She could not swim. The water took her all the way down here from the *"colonia"* upstream. But," He paused for emphasis. "A miracle happened. The baby was in God's hands. He sent an angel to guard it. It was still alive. That is the way of God. It is a way we don't always understand."

Steve and I had been surprised by this ending. We thought the story was over. This must have been the happy ending. Then Francisco continued:

"Here in *Choluteca*, it was bad. This *hacienda*," he motioned to the buildings behind us. "was six feet under water. One waitress had to be rescued from the roof. The whole valley was under water. The water was up to the level of the bridge.

"I knew it was bad. I had to come to work. My job is to guard the *hacienda*. It doesn't matter if it is raining. I told my wife, 'Get out of the house. Go to the hills with the others.' But she would not leave her house, her things, me.

"While I was at work, the waters rose. They took the house. They took my wife and one son."

Steve and I were shocked. We had not expected the misery and sadness of the story to strike so close to the story teller. We had nothing to say. I wiped away a tear and turned back to Francisco. He knew we were touched and saddened. He tried to make us feel better.

"But things are getting better." He straightened his gun belt and turned to watch a car leave the parking lot.

"We have had help. Help came from Canada and the US and Mexico. But no help came from our own country. It was too bad here. Help came from others. I have recovered. I have this job. It is enough. I have rice and beans and tortillas. I have God to comfort me. That is enough. It is all I need."

There is so little one can say to someone who has lost so much, someone who has seen others lose as much and more. What do you need to say to someone who has come to terms with life in his own way? There was nothing to be said.

The story stayed with us as we moved through the rest of the evening. We had tuna sandwiches as there had been no turkey to create leftovers. I was cleaning up and noticed Steve had put one of his sandwiches into a baggie and was headed for the door.

"I think I'll see if Francisco is in the mood for tuna." He said as he slipped out. It made me smile.

"My function in life was to render clear what was already blindly conspicuous."
Quintin Crisp

Chapter 22

Lost in the Mist

The mists on the mountaintops of Central America hid everything. Visibility was limited to 25 feet in any direction. Beyond that, all was lost in the white-out.

Thanks to our investment in good maps and guide books, we were never lost for very long. We had successfully made our way through Mexico, Belize, Guatemala, Honduras and Nicaragua. Frustration with the roads, the local style of driving, poorly researched maps, and each other had become an everyday experience. We learned to adjust to things. We even learned what to expect from our different styles of problem-solving and handling stress. Missing road signs were commonplace. Poorly described intersections were to be expected. We knew better than to expect the same answer to questions that were asked of three different locals. It all made sense in the montage that we had come to know as Central America. But now, something much larger and more dramatic than a road sign was lost for weeks at a time. The volcanoes of Nicaragua and Costa Rica were regularly lost in the mists.

The volcanoes rise majestically above the jungle-covered hills. We visited *Volcán Masaya* in Nicaragua, *Rincon de la Vieja* and *Volcán Arenal* in Costa Rica.

Stromboli-type volcanic cones reach steeply toward the sky. Three fourths of the way up their sides rests the "cloud line." Some of the cloud is generated by the volcanoes themselves. Gray clouds of sulfurous gases spewed from the volcanoes in a constant billowing stream. This constant reminder of the volcanoes' power joined with clouds that swept over the nearby ridges, up the sides and around the pointed tops of the mountains. It obscured everything except their jungle-covered shoulders. The volcanoes were like upside down icebergs. You could see their bases, but hidden behind the clouds were the tops, unknown and mysterious.

Looking down into the crater of *Volcán Masaya* in Nicaragua, the sheer cliffs caused you to catch your breath. The unseen but imagined depth of the crater was frightening. The edges where you stood were abrupt and ragged. From deep within the crater, huge 300-foot tall clouds of gasses issued. You never saw the bottom, which was completely obscured by the self-produced toxic cloud.

The gas clouds are potentially harmful to humans and other living creatures. Cars are all parked in the "get-away-position" just in case the winds shifted and sent toxic rain over the gawking visitors and their vehicles. If you made a *"gringo"* mistake and pulled in to a parking spot in the normal fashion, head in, the park ranger ran quickly to your window, tapped on the glass and commanded you to turn around *"immediamente, por favor."* They were serious about the possibility of a gas eruption. You could feel the hairs on your arms stand up as you realized you were teetering on the edge of a natural disaster, an imminent eruption, and a life-threatening incident. For us, it was adventure. For the locals it was everyday life.

Steve took the adventure of our visit to a live volcano one step further. He began a conversation with the same ranger that had advised us to park in the get-away position. Soon he was on a guided tour of one of the lava tubes that spiraled through the volcano's sides. I was not much of a cave person then, and to this day get the creeps from the idea of going deep into the bowels of the earth, just feet from a potential source of hot molten rock. Just a personal quirk, I guess. I had this wish to grow old and die in my bed somewhere, not be burned alive in a black rock cave, deep within the ground in a foreign country.

For Steve, this was the perfect opportunity. Walking in a cave combined two things he loved, hiking and caves. In the cave he saw swarms of bats hanging from the ceiling, crapping on the floors and squeaking at the intrusions of the humans. When evening fell, the bats looked forward to flying in huge undulating swarms out over the countryside around the volcano, settling on some unsuspecting cow or deer and drinking their nightly meal of fresh blood. No, I was quite happy to wait in the van and watch the clouds of poisonous gas billow out of the slumbering volcano, ready to pull away, with or without Steve.

Rincon de la Vieja volcano in Costa Rica was much harder to view up close. The hike to the crater required a sleep-over on the trail. Given the 40-mph winds and constant rainy mist, it was not an overnight I was willing to make. The mountaintop was always obscured from view by the clouds which spilled over the dividing mountain range of Central America. The clouds joined with the volcano's spewing cloud and then, caught by the fierce winds, slammed down the side of the mountain in a wet, howling rage.

Rincon kept its secrets well hidden with all this inaccessibility. Its environment was harsh and constant battering winds assaulted would-be visitors. Hints of its power and fury were revealed on the lower levels of the mountainside. Slate gray mud-pots bubbled and spurted. Steam vents filled the air with rotten egg smells and hot drifting steam. Hot springs dotted the mist covered-mountainside and blended with the water from the mists to create rushing creeks and crashing waterfalls.

The forbidding weather conditions protected wildlife and scenery. As we hiked through the temperate jungles on the volcano's sides we saw monkeys swinging from the trees. Butterflies with brilliant colors danced in and out of the mottled under story. Birds and small animals scurried in the tree tops, the tangled vines, and the fallen trees that lined the trail. Water barreled through the jungle as if late for a date with civilization in the towns far below. Then, unexpectedly, the water slipped silently into a hidden lava tube and disappeared completely from view. On one side of the trail was a rushing creek and on the other side was dry jungle and no water at all. It was a jungle filled with life and mystery.

Our next stop on the volcano circuit was *Arenal*, Costa Rica. We arrived at *Las Lagos* Park on the shoulder of *Volcán Arenal* after a two hour crawl around *Lago Arenal*. The pothole filled road we took to get there had crept through tropical rainforest. Mists kept the environment wet and the windshield wipers running. Streams cascaded over, under, and around the road. The trip was slow, bone jarring, exciting and beautiful. You had the feeling that few people had traveled this way. Who would go where roads were often washed out or turned to mud by the daily downpours and mists? The scenery was filled with unexpected views of the lake, glimpsed through openings in the tropical vegetation. Everything was a vibrant green, glistening with the falling mists.

From *Las Lagos* Park we looked toward what we imagined to be the volcano. It was lost in the mist. Our imaginations could not construct its shape or its volume. We would have to wait for the mountain to reveal itself. While we waited, we explored the wonders of the park-like resort. Since we were traveling on-the-cheap, we were parked in a flat graded-off area set aside for tent campers and hikers. Our 20-year old van looked like luxury compared to the soggy tents that our neighbors occupied. The resort offered cozy upscale bungalows to those with money to spend, a thermal heated pool and spa, lots of waterfalls and ponds fed by the constant rains, all with a surprising range of inhabitants.

Set on terraces on the hillside were ponds filled with talapia. These fish were raised for human food and as food for the other residents of the resort, the alligators. Spread throughout the resort were fenced-in areas, usually featuring a murky pond and a muddy bank. The ponds were inhabited by alligators of various sizes. They tried to keep the alligators grouped together in similar sizes to discourage them from eating their roommates. The resident alligators ranged from about 12 inches long to 8 feet long. Apparently they could grow even bigger, but became meat and handbags at that size. It was something to be thankful for. We were also happy they were raising the tilapia to feed these monsters.

Through the misty shroud that surrounded the resort we heard the mountain speaking. It told all who listened of its power, its potential to destroy anything in its path. Its most recent eruption was less than two years prior to our visit. It left a trail of new lava rock and buried campsites and houses. Now the mountain popped. It rumbled like thunder. It growled like a jet plane taking off in the mist. It filled the misty jungle with sounds, and then left you with silence, and a sense of expectancy.

Our first morning on the mountain was gray and rainy. By midday, the clouds parted and blue sky appeared. There, looming above us, larger than we had ever imagined, was the mountain. It was uncomfortably close. If it had chosen to erupt while we were there visiting, we could easily have become one of the permanent features of the landscape, encapsulated in the molten rock that bubbled and groaned inside the mountain.

A perfect cone shape, half the mountain was black with recent lava flows. Lava crept out of cracks continually, producing feathery clouds of misty sulfur. The other half of the mountain was covered in dense jungle. The dividing line between the two was a fringe of trees, felled in one direction. They looked like so many bare matchsticks, lifeless and burned, struck down by the recent lava flow.

Steam and gas clouds poured from the twin craters. The cracks and vents along the recent lava flows fumed and steamed. At night these are said to glow red, giving a glimpse of the mountain's inner fury.

Lost in the Mist

While we were lucky to see the volcano clearly, hear its rumbling and grumbling, we were not privileged to see the nighttime lava show. As evening approached, the clouds blew across the mountainside, joined with sulfur clouds and *Volcán Arenal* was once again lost in the mist.

> "Sometimes peace is simply defined as the absence of stress!"
> Karen McGinnis

Chapter 23

The Wind God of the Rincon

As New Year's approached we searched for a place that would give us peace and quiet, beautiful views and an interesting environment to explore. *Rincon de la Vieja* National Park in Costa Rica met every requirement.

It was 25 kilometers off of the main road. The access road was dirt, rocks, gravel and ruts. The park was perched on the side of a volcano, just below the crest of Costa Rica's dividing mountain range. The unobstructed views from the parking lot reached all the way to the ocean. The park itself was laced with trails that led through dry tropical forests to the edges of sputtering volcanic mud pots, steaming sulfur-scented vents, hot water pools, waterfalls, streams that disappeared into lava tubes and active volcanoes. What the guide books failed to mention was that this was the domain of the wind god of the Rincon. We found that out the hard way.

The setting sun cast long shadows on the volcanic landscape that lay between its fiery evening glow and our mountainside perch. Volcanic peaks, cinder cones, lava flow ridges and sediment filled valleys and reflected the suns fading rays. Gradually all the features melted together into a blue-black backdrop for the twinkling city lights below.

A brisk breeze blew down the face of the mountain. We were grateful for that breeze. It meant the vicious, biting black gnats could not navigate their way onto our waiting skin. The bug nets that we had jerry-rigged onto every opening of our van were in place. The gnats were almost small enough to fit through the mesh. They struggled at the openings, the buzzing of thousands of tiny bodies kept up a constant threat of pain and suffering. Our hearts went out to the tent campers and backpackers who were sitting outside by fires and sleeping in the open air on the ground. The breeze was a blessing that spared all of us the half inch welts with bright bleeding centers that represented the successful bite of these gnats. The winds of the Rincon seemed beneficent. We were mistaken.

We thought the breeze kept away the mists that appeared at the crest of the mountain range. Caught in the wind, these clouds just blew apart. They became little more than a refreshing sprinkle on the faces of trail-weary hikers. We thought the wind was keeping us cool and refreshed, nothing more. We were wrong.

We began to realize our error when the van began rocking, then, jerking violently from side to side. Not gentle, breezy rocking that lulls you to sleep. It was violent, jolting jerks, like rioters trying to overturn cars, like being hit broadside by a truck, unexpectedly. The hanging

The Wind God of the Rincon

overhead lamp in our van began swinging crazily and never stopped.

Gusts forced the bug screens off the open windows. The duct tape we had used to hold them in place was no match for the wind. Then the force of the wind demanded we close the windows. We were captives of the wind. Sunset had been a time of awakening for the wind god of the Rincon. Now he was exacting a heavy price for his benevolence during the daylight hours.

After a hard day of hiking on the trail, time for "lights out" came early. We were closed up in the van, captives, with little to do but wait, watch and listen to the wrath, or was it the mischief, of the wind.

The wind whistled around the storage box on the roof rack. It creaked. It groaned. It shuddered. Was it shut tight? Locked and secured to the rack? Had the wind and the rough gravel road loosened the bolts and made it a potential play toy for the wind? Steve braved the elements, which by now included horizontally blowing rain, and checked the box. One tie down was cinched up a little tighter, and then he blew back into the van with a blast of cold, wet air. The wind and rain rushed into the van ahead of him like a spirit and filled every corner with its presence.

Now the wind crept under the van and lifted it. The frame groaned. Then it dropped it. The agony of the van was almost human as it shuddered and settled. Were we parked on an unstable surface? Would the rock pavement beneath us give way, leaving us a tumbling mass of camp stoves, hiking clothes and folding chairs?

Wait! Why were we so paranoid? Of course we were parked on stable ground. It was a parking lot. Vans don't just tip over in the wind. Or do they? We ran through these thoughts and more a hundred times as the wind tipped and rocked and shook our sanctuary.

As the night wore on, the force of the wind ebbed and flowed around the van. It beat against the front grill, then reversed itself and rattled the tailgate. Then after a few minutes of deafening stillness, it hit the right side, streaked under and blew up the opposite side of the van. Then after a moment's hesitation, it slammed again into the storage box. The van was in a constant state of motion.

If we had been in a cabin on a sail boat and it was 'blowing stink' like this outside, I would have seriously considered the possibility of rounding down before the force of the gale. We would have been in danger of going over into the waves, mast into the water and all hands on deck dumped out into the sea. But we were stuck in the van on the side of the mountain and there was no port to make for, no SOS to send, no sails to reef, no hatches to batten.

We played our only card and that was to wait. I waited for sleep to come and block out the rocking and rolling. Steve, ever vigilant, fell instantly into the sleep of the exhausted. I waited for morning to come and end the darkness that swirled angrily around us. I waited for whatever was going to happen. This was a New Year's that I would never forget. New Year's Eve is supposed to be a time of reflection and appreciation. It is a time to make resolutions for the future and marvel over where you've been and what

The Wind God of the Rincon

you've accomplished. As I lay there, rocking and rolling through the night, I reflected, I appreciated and I marveled. My resolution was to never have an experience like this again.

The forces of nature played around us. The wind god exacted his due. And all the while, the earth continued turning and morning finally came. Our little yellow van greeted the rising sun, safe and secure in the parking lot. We emerged, bleary-eyed, with a new respect for the forces of nature on the Rincon.

"One may go a long way after one is tired."
French Proverb

Chapter 24

How to Ship a Van

We arrived in Panama clearly focused on our objective: ship the van to South America. Our eight days in the country were devoted almost entirely to accomplishing this task.

The challenge of making this happen had been hanging over our heads for almost a year. Very little current information was available. Books in print were out of date and inaccurate. Most still referred to US military presence in the Canal Zone or the ferry to Colombia. Neither still existed. Even the internet had little current information.

We had gathered a pile of names, numbers, and bits of hearsay, advice and warnings. Now the fat was in the fire and we would have to separate fact from fiction and make shipping the van a reality.

Our first step was to decide what to do about Colombia. The country had literally been shooting itself in the foot as far as tourists were concerned. Kidnappings, murders and car bombings were not very inviting to the average traveler. Most embassies advised their citizens to avoid traveling to Colombia. We met a Belgian family who had been living in Colombia. The wife clearly stated, "It is a beautiful country, but you can't travel there." She and her husband brought their own children to Costa Rica to see the jungle and animals. Even they did not travel within Colombia.

The Darien Gap further influenced our decision to avoid Colombia. All maps indicated a gap of over 100 miles between parts of Panama and Colombia. The dirt track through the jungle has been traversed by travelers on foot and bicycle, and by other hearty souls who lived on the edge. We did not fit that description. There were rumors of people riding and carrying off-road motorcycles through the jungle. Taking our van through was not physically possible despite what *La Dueña* had written on her itinerary in Chapter 2.

We chose to ship our van to Ecuador. It was the next closest country, had a reputation for spectacular scenery, great monetary exchange, and accommodating inhabitants.

I called every shipping agency in the phone book, Lonely Planet Guide, South American Explorers Club guides, and all the names listed on bits and pieces of materials we had gathered. We narrowed it down to three. Prices ranged from $950USD to $1200USD. We picked a mid-range company and made a lucky choice. The shipping company and their agents performed efficiently and personably.

The rest of the process was a little more stressful. Steve spent five hours in the PTJ (*Policia Tecnica Judicial*) office. He emerged with one piece of paper releasing the van from the country. During the five hours he was in the PTJ office, I waited in the van, parked in a questionable part of town, watching would-be thieves glance my way.

The process Steve endured involved only one police official. As the only one in all of Panama with the authority to produce this document, he was obviously over-worked, and under-supported by one secretary who typed 20 words per minute on a manual typewriter. To make the experience even more memorable, the official chose to share the part of his personality that resembled cold oatmeal mush with any and all who came to see him. This was a perfect example of when and where not to be an ugly American. Just the right amount of pressure and patience was required. Like the plane in Guatemala that was overbooked, one had to know how to maintain a place in line, and as in the many border crossings, a certain amount of innocence was required to melt any arrogance or superiority that many expected of American travelers. Steve walked a tightrope of composure.

The trip to the Customs Office with the paper created by the PTJ (pronounced pay-tay-ho-tay) was just as nerve-racking. Just getting to the office was a challenge. Streets in Panama City were not clearly marked, if marked at all. Many were under repair. This meant maps were inaccurate. What looked to be a straight shot on the map turned out to be a maze of one-way streets, all going the wrong way, and blocked intersections filled with ditches, construction equipment and traffic police motioning you in the opposite direction from the way you wanted to go?

One stop at a neighborhood police station illustrated this point. After hours of hopelessly trying to follow our map and instructions given to us by helpful locals, we were hopelessly lost. One option was to melt down and self-destruct. We chose to ask for help. We had seen a small police outpost on one of our wrong turns. We returned to that spot, desperate for directions. Four uniformed officers tried to help us. One gave up and said "You cannot reach this destination from where you are now." We had trouble processing the lack of logic in that statement. No one from North America could even imagine saying that to someone seeking directions. There is always a way to get "there" from "here." However, this was Panama and a Latin American country. No one here wanted to tell us that they did not know how to get "there", had never been to a customs office, or had any idea what the condition of the roads was between where we were and where we wanted to go. We finally just asked the officers for their "best guess" and assured them we would not hold them responsible if we got lost again. The watch commander finally sent us blindly driving, by faith alone, in the right direction.

We arrived at the customs office on the run. We feared we had come too late. If PTJ had taken five hours, how long would this take?

Many employees were leaving as we were entering. This was a bad sign. We caught the processor as she was gathering her purse to leave. We must have looked pathetic. She chose to stay and help us. The cashier had, however, already left. Who else would take our $4US for the "Permission to Ship" papers? Without this paper we could not ship our van. Four dollars and a few minutes

How to Ship a Van

time stood between us and the possibility of successfully parting with all our worldly goods at the shipping dock.

After leading us through two other offices in search of help, the clerk took us to the desk of the Regional Administrator of Customs. By now we were really scared, tired and truly humble. These people held the fate of our van and our airline reservations in their hands. The van was due to ship at 8AM the next day. Customs opened again at 8:30AM. The drive between the two points was 2 hours long. We tried to do the math logically, but kept coming out short on time and low on luck. Without this paper, we were screwed.

The Administrator also took pity on us and gave permission to create the necessary paper. We would then pay the $4 the next afternoon. We received the permission paper and spent the night sleeplessly wondering what the next day held. How early did we need to leave Panama City to make it to the shipping office on time? Would there be traffic? Would we get lost again and arrive late? The variables were beyond counting and out of our control. We had considered camping out at the shipping office to assure that we would arrive on time. The shipping office was at the port which had a horrible reputation. It was a toss-up as to whether we were taking a bigger risk to sleep overnight in a bad part of town or run the risk of traffic and trying to reach the office on time.

We chose to stay in Panama City and risk the traffic in the morning. Even that was not easy. We could not park our van safely in the city and there were no campgrounds listed. We stayed at a downtown hotel that offered inside parking. We soon discovered that we would have to remove the storage box off of the top of our van in order to park in the inside parking. The valet parking manager assured us that the van would fit into the garage opening. We had our doubts. Steve convinced him that we should drive the van into the garage. As Steve inched his way toward the doorway, I watched to see if there was clearance. Just as the van reached the doorway, the cement driveway dipped at an angle to drop into the underground parking. At that exact spot, the storage box came in contact with the frame of the opening. As onlookers watched and offered useless advice, Steve and I unloaded the storage box, removed the box from the roof, placed it in the van, repacked it, removed the racks, put them in the van and then drove into the parking garage. The experience gave a whole new definition to the term frustration. We were beyond exhausted. If we had not been so anxious about making it to the shipping office on time, we would have slept like babies.

The next morning our shipping agent walked us through the maze of inspections, fees, and offices at the port. One step included a visit by a drug-sniffing dog. The K-9 police officer took one look at the cramped interior of our 20-year old van and waved us on. The dog never came close to our smelly vehicle, although other cars were thoroughly sniffed.

The van fit snuggly into the twenty-foot container. Chalked under each wheel and tied to the interior from every direction, the doors were locked and sealed. It was on its way. Time lapsed since our arrival at the shipping office: four hours.

We had bonded with our shipping agent during the eight days in Panama and the four hours at the port. As we parted he said he wanted to give us something special to

How to Ship a Van

take with us on our trip. There in the middle of the busy shipping company office, he held both our hands, and prayed aloud to God that we would stay safe over the next 6 1/2 months of traveling. After the experiences of the last four months, this blessing was one of the best parting gifts we could have received. We knew the value of having someone watching out for you. We needed all the help we could get.

We left the office relieved of the burden of uncertainty about getting the vehicle to South America. It was on its way. We were $1127USD poorer due to freight fees, but felt somehow richer for the experience.

Our shipping agent then made sure we were safely on the correct bus to the airport and out of the rundown, lawless shipping district.

Next challenge: pick up the van in Guayaquil, Ecuador.

"You never know when you are making a memory."
Rickie Lee Jones
"Young Blood"

Chapter 25

A Walking Tour of Quito

From Panama we flew to Quito, Ecuador to spend the time waiting for our van to arrive by ship in the port of Guayaquil. Big cities are not my thing, and as the capital of Ecuador, Quito was a big city. As of January 2000, Quito had 1.2 million people and counting. While it was a big city, it did have redeeming qualities.

At an elevation of 2850 meters (times 3.2 for the metrically challenged), or 9,120 feet, my back pack full of tank tops and shorts was a big mistake. It was not hot, even though it was located smack-dab on the Equator. In fact, due to the elevation, it was downright cold. The art of layering clothes definitely came in handy for our walking tour of Quito.

Our first walk took us through Quito´s lovely parks. In the New Town, *Parque El Ejido* sat amid streets clogged with buses, trolleys, honking taxis and scurrying private cars. Its rolling knolls offered a sunny place to observe the gathering mob of strikers protesting the 75% increase in transportation costs. Nearby, craftspeople sold their wares, unconcerned about the loudspeakers blaring political slogans or the waving banners.

Closer to the town's colonial center sat a pie-shaped chunk of park called *La Alameda*. Here, Simon Bolivar was immortalized in bronze, forever leading the people of South America to a better life. That struggle to survive and thrive was still very real.

At *Plaza de Independencia* in the heart of the Old Town, carefully manicured flowers and privet hedges flourished behind sculpted cement walls. Even on a Friday morning, the park was filled with strollers, talkers, families, tourists and police. Quaintly costumed guards graced the porch of the *Palacio Gobierno* (Government Palace). Camouflage-clad soldiers lounged nearby, equipped with tear gas canisters and launchers, and supported by armored troop carriers. We were admonished for taking pictures. Apparently they did not want anyone outside to know just how tenuous things were in Ecuador.

The walk through the Old Town brought many surprises. The colonial buildings were charming. The cobbled streets were narrow. Most buildings were well preserved, and painted in soft colors, sported tile roofs and wrought iron balconies with bright flowers. Women watched from balconies as life went by on the street below.

The market stalls which clogged many of these streets offered a wide variety of clothing, food and manufactured goods. Handicrafts were scarce here. Pickpockets, however, were readily available. While I was separated from Steve by two female accomplices, a young man tried to inspect the interior of my empty, zippered pockets. He got a resounding backhand across the chest for his efforts and a loud lecture in Spanish. He was shocked to hear this "*gringa*" unleash a torrent of Spanish. He beat a hasty retreat while his two female accomplices tried to distract Steve from calling the police.

Dozens of dramatic cathedrals and basilicas graced the city. Their ornate exteriors sported gargoyles, buttressed spires and huge carved doors. The gilded interiors were equally ornate, lit by stained glass windows and candles. They were frequented by the faithful. Two cathedrals we visited had Mass in progress and shared their peaceful ambiance with us, two street-weary walkers. After the press of the crowds in the market place and the encounter with the pickpockets, this respite truly felt like a visiting a sanctuary.

We planned ahead when we wanted to walk in the evenings. We surveyed the other travelers at our *pension*. Was anyone going out? Could we all go together? Several female travelers were always eager to take up our invitation to hit the streets together. Walking at night for single females was playing a game of strolling roulette. We chose our walking route carefully. We went directly from our *pension* to the lighted part of town and immediately entered the business and restaurant section. This was the safest area for tourists as it was surrounded by well-lit parks, busy streets and high rise hotels. Some travelers who were not so cautious found themselves waylaid, beaten, robbed and left alone on the sidewalk.

For meals we chose the restaurant section of New Town. The wide modern streets were filled with the smell of foods from around the world. Curry and ginger mingled with cilantro. *Fritado* (fried meat and potato) beckoned to the locals and repulsed visiting vegetarians.

We chose a *"typica"* cafe on the *Avenida Amazona*. Our meal selection was a mixed grill plate with delicious *llapingachos*. These crispy fried potato pancakes had a filling of tangy cheese. Delicious! The meal was large enough for two to share and cost $3.20 USD. Another of the charms of Quito.

The walk home through the brisk night air helped work off some of the calories we had consumed. Latin rhythms filled the air. Cigarette smoke and the smell of local and imported beers wafted from open *cantina* doorways. The streets, discos, bar and cafes of Quito were alive until the not-so-wee hours of the morning. We often left our dinner companions to dance the night away and take a taxi home as we strolled back arm-in-arm through the crisp night air.

Our next morning walk took us to the trio of museums called the *Casa de Cultura*. Housed in one huge round, modern building were three museums. Their focus was on the art of Ecuador since 1830, the clothing of the indigenous people, and the native-made instruments of the country. They brought the culture within easy reach. Clothing of the people clearly reflected their environment. High altitude tribes favored heavy woven woolens and many layers of clothing. Amazonian tribes needed only necklaces, wrist and anklets of beads made from shells and nut husks, and very little else...perhaps a loosely woven strip of plant fiber cloth for special occasions. I felt as though we had walked through the many cultural zones of the country.

The best part of the walking tours was the exercise. We had discovered a great bakery just across from the *Parque El Ejido* and quickly became addicted. Thirty-five cent French pastries and caramel Napoleons had our names written all over them. They were so rich that we would have had to walk completely around Quito everyday just to work off the calories. After months of no desserts and bland meals, we enjoyed our stay in Quito to the fullest. Just around the corner from the bakery was a small hole-in-the-wall restaurant that offered a three-course lunch for $1.50USD. It was the perfect place to sit, eat, and watch the military police throw tear gas canisters at the demonstrators as they marched through the streets.

Without the opportunity to walk through Quito's parks, churches, markets and museums, we would surely have taken home more weighty reminders of our visit than just our memories.

> *"There is always room at the top."*
> English Proverb

Chapter 26

Everybody Needs a Bus Monkey

He clung to the roof rack, grabbing at luggage and bulging bags of un-shucked corn. He hung onto the side of the moving bus with one hand and at every stop, he chattered a stream of incomprehensible gibberish to potential passengers. He pulled them on board until every seat was filled.

He was a bus monkey.

We first noticed and came to appreciate bus monkeys in Mexico and Central America. They could be observed crawling up and down the sides of moving buses, deftly hoisting the possessions of passengers to the roof, then securing them while the still-moving bus jolted and bounced over the roads were the term "paved" mostly meant "not dirt."

We had minimal contact with bus monkeys and saw them as merely agile additions to the transportation system. They were a convenience for passengers with oversized luggage, or for those who needed help exiting a crowded bus through the emergency exit at the rear. His job was to help. His flying fingers and acrobatic tendencies made all these tasks look simple, effortless.

On the 8 ½ hour bus ride from Quito to Guayaquil, Ecuador, we came to understand the role and value of the bus monkey more clearly. We had not expected to have a bus monkey on this trip, as we were taking the first-class bus and not the general public transit bus. But what we got was a first-class bus monkey, complete with dress slacks, white shirt and tie. This was a professional bus monkey, the best in the business.

At the first stop, the public terminal, he cruised the competing bus line parking areas, calling out the names of the major stops along our route. Six or eight passengers joined our ranks, abandoning the other bus lines.

At every stop, crossroads or gathering of people along the road, he leaned out, secured to the bus by one hand and one foot.

"Santo Dominto-Quevado-Babahoyo-Quayaquil." He called, all in one breath.

One or two passengers jumped on here, four more there, and soon the bus was filled.

Now came the time for money to change hands. The bus monkey had filled the seats, now he must remember when each passenger got on, what percentage of the full fare each would pay, and then collect that amount. Money was paid by hands full of crumpled paper notes and small coins. The bus monkey deftly made correct change, either immediately, or as he collected the proper denominations from other passengers. His mind worked like a computer. The bus monkey remembered who owed what, who paid what and who got what change. He never missed a single customer or made an error in making change. No passenger rode free. No one complained about the fare.

If passengers got off, his recruiting process began again until every seat was filled. Fee adjustments were made and the toll collected on the spot.

We came to understand that the bus monkey was the secret to running an efficient and economically viable bus line. He was a promoter, a marketing manager, a salesman. Through his efforts, every passenger had his needs met, luggage handled, and reached the correct destination.

Perhaps his most important role was to eliminate stress for the driver. The driver was free to concentrate on the narrow, windy mountain road, the sudden appearance of slow, or non-moving trucks in the road ahead, rocks or animals on the roadway, or any other impediments to the safe and timely progress of the bus.

In short, the bus monkey was just the kind of employee every business needed for promotion, maximization of profits and efficiency. We haven't even mentioned the entertainment value of having a bus monkey on board. His lively antics and efficiency would brighten any business owner's day just as he filled our long journey with activity and made the time fly by.

> *"The first and great commandment is:
> don't let them scare you!"*
> Elmer Davis

Chapter 27

Retrieving a Van

Retrieving the van from its destination port in Ecuador was an experience closely resembling a root canal or an IRS audit. Under the best of conditions it was over quickly and was only mildly painful like a root canal. Under the worst of conditions it seemed to drag on endlessly and it was impossible to predict the ultimate outcome until it was over, just like an audit.

Our trial by paperwork was delayed a week. Our van which had been carefully scheduled, container-ized, and was dutifully awaiting loading at the port of *Manzanillo* in Panama, was not loaded as planned. It sat for a week on the dock because the boat it was to be shipped on arrived too late to take on new freight and had to rush to meet its scheduled Canal crossing. We kept thinking of how we stressed and jumped through hoops to make sure the van was at the port at exactly the appointed time.

The shipping company handled all the paperwork for the change while we enjoyed the culture and cuisine of Quito, Ecuador. The miracle of email saved us from cutting that visit short and rushing to the port of Guayaquil, Ecuador to await the arrival of the van on its original schedule. We also avoided the highway road blocks created by striking Ecuadorians who placed burning trees and boulders on the roads in protest of a 75% increase in bus fares by the government. We found flexibility, patience and an ability not to know all the details of how, why and when regarding the arrival of our van to be an asset.

Instead of rushing to Guayaquil, we took *Salsa* and Spanish lessons in Quito. We visited the local art shows and open markets. We were terrible at *Salsa*, apparently having been born without rhythm. I believe our instructors were relieved that we finally had to leave and stop taking lessons. *"Un, dos, tres."* They repeated this endlessly, urging us to step forward on the *"Un."* and to swivel non-swiveling hips to the music. We sweated and tried and laughed, but left, still rhythmically challenged and *Salsa*-less. The only salsa we were good at was the variety that came in a dish featuring chopped tomatoes and cilantro.

Our Spanish lessons were somewhat more successful. As *Norteameicanos* we were somewhat more cerebral than we were rhythmic. We enjoyed the one-on-one conversation with our patient Ecuadorian teacher. We even developed enough vocabulary to engage in some abstract discussions about the state of political affairs in the country.

Things were not good. The poor were disenfranchised and the rich ran the country. The gap that separated them grew wider with the increasing bus fares, a mode of transportation used by the majority of the poor people. Imagine that the cost of gas for your car increased by 75% overnight. The response of the local people in Quito was to

Retrieving a Van

hold demonstrations in the parks, roll burning tires down onto traffic that passed below on narrow mountain roads, and generally make life miserable for everyone. We saw the country rapidly descending into chaos and hoped our van would arrive soon. We kept a low profile, avoided the tear gas in the streets and made sure not to be out of our hotel after dark.

We were notified by email that our van had shipped from Panama and was due to arrive in the port of Guayaquil. We were instructed when and where to check-in to receive the van. We arrived *"en punto"*, on time, at the shipping office in Guayaquil once our van was actually in port. We then learned that *"en punto"* meant not having to wait more than an hour and a half to receive the correct bill of lading and meet the private customs agent we were hiring. Our agent turned out to be a dapper older gentleman named Guillermo de Franc. We found out how much "older" our agent was when in conversation he revealed his age. He was 82. They must count time differently below the equator as he looked 60 and ran around the port like a 20-year old. He left us puffing and sweating in his dust. He and his family provided us with meals, cold drinks, comfort, and Kleenex for drying tears when times ahead got rough.

Every single moment of the five days we dealt with Customs in Ecuador can be described as "hurry up and wait." We made the trip to and from the port helter-skelter through the busy city streets, with SR. de Franc driving at top speed. Imagine a real life video game where you race to your destination while taxis and buses appear unexpectedly, cut you off, turn or stop in front of you, and pedestrians appear at any moment as they attempt to cross a six lane boulevard. Peering intently through his thick glasses, SR. de

Franc negotiated it all. Passages from "Mr. Toad's Wild Ride" kept flashing through my mind as I grasped the door handle and braced myself in the back seat of his tiny car.

The "wait" part occurred at the Custom's office. Ecuador wanted an insurance paper called a Carnet de Passage or *triptico*. This guarantees you will leave their country with your vehicle. This type of "insurance" was not sold in the US, but only through third-party countries such as Canada. It was not sold in Ecuador. It provided insurance only to the host country at a price of around $700. It only covered the event of a car being sold within the country, and the beneficiary was the host country itself. We had not purchased it and did not have any way to purchase it now that we were in Ecuador. This was a classic example of Catch 22. This is the point where the experience changed from root canal (with *triptico*) to audit (without *triptico*).

There was another insurance option. You could obtain a "guarantee" from your Embassy that you will leave the country with your car. Yeh, right! No American is even momentarily foolish enough to believe our government was in the business of guaranteeing our actions thousands of miles from home, completely unenforceable. No embassy would issue this letter.

We were as close to having a guarantee letter as anyone could get. While in Quito, we visited the US Embassy where local-boy-gone-international, Mike Hoff, was the General Services Officer. He was a former home-room classmate of mine in high school. It was a small world. He and his office provided us with an official letter, on letter head, with seal and signature, stating we were not in Ecuador to sell our van, but were tourists traveling

Retrieving a Van

throughout South America and returning to the US with the vehicle. An almost word-for-word copy of this letter had been issued by other embassies and used by Swiss and Canadian travelers within the last two months with success.

Our letter caused considerable head scratching at the custom's office in Guayaquil. The buck was passed from office to office. No one was willing to make a decision as to whether or not the letter was acceptable. We waited and waited at each office. Finally it was sent to the *Advisario de Aduana* (advising lawyer's office) who issued an official or "safe" interpretation. Since the letter never actually used the word "guarantee" in it, it was useless. We could not enter the country with the vehicle for more than 24 hours and an officer of the Custom's Service (police) must accompany us directly to the border. In plain language, we were given 24 hours to get out of the country under armed guard!

Since the only other alternative was to give the customs office a certified (not personal) check for the value of the car, this police escort actually sounded pretty good. Our agent tried everything he had learned in his 50 years of experience to soften the verdict. Could he accompany us instead of the police? No. Could he give them his local, personal check? After all he was a licensed agent of the Customs Service and a businessman for over 50 years? No.

At least we all knew where we stood in the eyes of the Customs Service. We were just short of criminals whose intent was to pay to ship a 20-year old van to Ecuador, then sell it and completely upset their country's delicate economic balance. Seems unlikely, but that was their view.

The next challenge was to actually find the van. The container it was in was numbered so it would seem a simple task to track it. Wrong. There were dozens of huge warehouses for each freight line and acres of storage lots where containers were stacked four high in seemingly endless rows. At one point we were told the van was out of the container. This was our worst nightmare. It was container-ized with the keys in it and would be sitting somewhere in the maze of warehouses and parking areas with the keys inside, unlocked. We envisioned a "Take me" sign plastered on the van, now filled with all our hard to replace possessions.

When I heard that this had happened to our van, I broke down in tears. Nothing in the van was worth much, but the thought of being stranded here, van-less after all we had been through just to be eligible to receive the van, was more than I could handle. The uncertainty, the pressure, the illogical responses, all came pouring over me and I melted into a puddle of sobs. Fortunately we were at SR. de Franc's house at the time this occurred. His wife and daughters comforted me, provided tissues, nodded understandingly, and glared at SR. de Franc for having put me in such a state with his inability to retrieve the van. It was just the impetus he needed. He shifted his efforts from high gear to overdrive.

After another wild ride to the port, we visited the Chief of Warehouses. He called every building. No one had the van. Since it could not be located in a warehouse, it must still be in a container. We left with a mustard seed of hope that this might be true. The next morning, driving past a storage lot, we actually spotted a container with our number on it. Thankfully while in Panama we had written down the

Retrieving a Van

name on the container and the identification number stamped on the end. It was found. Without Steve's eagle eye, the van might still be sitting in that shipping yard. The actual uncrating process was anticlimactic. The van was intact as were our possessions. More waiting and paperwork and we were released with a Customs Police escort to return to our hotel.

At first we saw this customs representative as a positive thing. His name was actually Angel Zapata (which almost translates to angel shoes?). We hoped he would speed the next part of the process along. Wrong. He turned out to be an angel with his hand out and very little idea how to accomplish his assigned task. Our first stop was at his compound for a signature to release him to take us to the border the next morning. We arrived at 6 PM to find his boss was in a meeting. At 9 PM Steve had grown tired of waiting, questioning, and inquiring as to the progress in obtaining the required signature. We firmly came to believe that Angel was inside the compound enjoying his dinner and chatting with friends while we waited at street side.

We decided I would play the bitch and kick up a fuss. It was amazing what a tall blond woman using a loud voice and bad high school Spanish could accomplish. Within 15 minutes I had been let into the security compound, found Zapata, obtained the signature from someone and we were on our way. Once again, had we not taken this action, we might still be sitting at the curb in front of the police barracks, waiting for something to happen.

Our experience with Zapata was not over yet. He negotiated his "fee" for accompanying us to the border. He wanted $40USD and a free night at the hotel, all meals and a bus ride back. We settled on $40USD only and he set the departure time at 5 AM. We arrived at the hotel, secured the van in the car park and bade him good night. He hesitated.

"You know," he said, "5AM is going to be too early for me to catch a bus." He wasn't worried about the bus schedule. He was fishing for us to pay for a taxi to get him from the customs compound to the hotel. He was surprised when this ploy for more money initiated a "no more nonsense" response from me, a school teacher.

"You set the time at 5 AM. Be here at 5 AM. Spend $2 on a taxi if you have to. Good night." I dismissed him and we left him standing bewildered on the sidewalk as we entered the hotel.

The night was filled with questions. Would he show up? Would he show up on time? What could we do if he didn't show up? How long should we wait? Would my "crazed woman" routine work again?

At 4:45 AM the room phone rang. Zapata was in the lobby. We were off. There was very little traffic at 5 AM and the trip to the border was uneventful. We arrived at the border crossing in time to tie up some loose ends like water, oil for the car and lunch.

At 2 PM we were still waiting for customs to reopen after their siesta. Zapata then discovered that, once again, the person needed for signatures was not there and no one knew when to expect him. Steve snapped. He got into the van and started in the direction of the border. As we crept through the packed street, we decided to try "woman

Retrieving a Van

power" one last time. What did we have to lose?

While Steve waited in the middle of the market-day street, I went into the Customs Office. There was Zapata, milling about in the office, doing nothing and talking to no one. With all the authority of a 5th grade teacher, I confronted him in front of secretaries and other customs police.

"We are heading for the border. Are you coming? You kept us waiting three hours the night before. You can not pull the same game again today." My Spanish was bad, but he understood perfectly and looked sheepish. From a back office a nicely dressed young man approached us. He took the papers from Zapata, reviewed them, and gave him a round of sharp questions. Politely asking me for a "little more patience", he beckoned for us both to follow him. We marched, single file through the teaming streets, with Steve following slowly behind in the van, creeping through the narrow opening between the market stalls and the milling shoppers. We created quite a little parade: a mid-level customs official, a customs policeman, a near-tears American woman and a bearded man driving a beat-up yellow VW campervan.

At a closet size office at the border, our papers were stamped in 5 or 6 places, signed, double signed, another set of copies made and we were done. The young official took us to the Peruvian Customs Office. He shook my hand, apologized for the "inconveniences" and disappeared. Angel Zapata appeared just long enough to retrieve the balance of his "fee" and also disappeared.

Steve entered the Peruvian Customs Office, fully expecting

the gauntlet to begin again. Surprise! They were friendly, even welcoming. They appeared to consider the Ecuadorians to be foolish people who had wasted a great deal of time. After all, all this trouble could scare away tourists. Everyone knows tourists want to see the country and spend a lot of money. Stamp. Stamp.

"Welcome to Peru," they said with a smile and a handshake.

> *"Courage is being scared to death,
> and saddling up anyway."*
> John Wayne

Chapter 28

The First Eight Days in Peru

We should have known Peru would be different from the other Latin American countries we visited. We entered under police escort. Now that was different, and just the beginning.

Our 12 hour marathon day of crossing the border ended and we settled into a guest house at Costa Blanca, Peru. We had only driven 15 minutes from the border, but the terrain had already changed dramatically. We had come from a muggy, humid jungle and now we were in desert. We settled down under some palms on the beach to lick our wounds and recover from our border crossing.

We were immediately adopted by the family of the owners. Lucho, the buoyant father figure with a bald head fringed by white hair, never stopped smiling. More than willing to help, he even went into town to purchase a 220V to 110V converter for us. This was a different attitude from what we had experienced in Ecuador. Rosana, his wife, proudly showed us the model's portfolio of her daughter, who was Miss Peru 2000. She held various other national beauty titles and was currently in, you guessed it, Hollywood. Gonzalo, the silent, long haired teenager, smiled, but said nothing for the five days we were with the family. Fernando "Nanu" was a nephew and the driving force of the family. He was an artist. Boats he sculpted from coconut shells and fronds delighted the neighborhood children. Drawings covered the walls of the living room. Songs he wrote, played and sang attracted guests, family, friends and townspeople to the resort area that his extended family owned. His biggest talent was his personality. His radiant smile made everyone he met an instant friend. Listening to his nonstop talk of the future, you believed that he would accomplish his goals, become a professional musician and travel to the United States.

Alas, all was not well in paradise. The day after arriving, I was attacked by a violent six hour bug. I could only attribute this illness to the dinner featuring raw *ceviche* that had been served for Steve's birthday. This was my first bout of illness in the four months of the trip. *Ojala!* God willing, it would be the only bout for the next six months as well. It left me weak and only able to respond to Rosana's nurturing care, jell-o, Sprite and Gatorade. Two planned days of R & R turned into five days of forced rest and recovery.

Though I was still weak in the knees, we hit the road to view the ruins of the Mochi pyramids. Time, wind, rain, *conquistadors* and grave robbers had worked their worst, and the once proud temples were reduced to eroded adobe hills. We spent the night at the side of the *policia national* guard's house at the site. They entertained us with *cumbia* music and loud conversations far into the night. We were safe, but not too rested.

The next pyramid site at Sipan was in no better condition, but the contents of the graves had been saved. They rivaled King Tut's tomb in Egypt for quantities of gold, silver and textiles. The archeologist-ticket taker there offered us yet another adventure at *Pampagrande*. This site was still under excavation. His excitement was contagious and we agreed to visit the site with him when he got off his shift.

His "15 minute drive" turned out to be more than an hour over dirt paved and pot hole-filled roads. Our first stop was a "discovery" he had made, but not yet shared with the world. After parking in someone's yard, crossing through a soccer game in progress and picking our way up a thorn-bush covered hillside, we approached his discovery. There on a huge bolder, partially dug out of the sandy hillside, was a drawing of a six foot tall figure. It had a perfectly round head, a navel, and six arms and legs.

"See how it is so similar to figures found in the East Indian culture?" Our guide asked. Having seen many other petroglyphs scattered across the Latin America and the southwestern United States, we were truly amazed at how much this resembled the drawings Steve had seen first hand in Asia and India. Amazed and perplexed. Was it original to the Mochi culture, or just original to the guide? We were not sure what kind of reaction he expected from us. We may have been too subdued or not impressed enough to suit him. We weren't archeologists, after all, just travelers.

After leaving the site we traveled on through a sugar cane village where the guide picked up his girlfriend. Things were beginning to get a little strange as we both remembered him telling us he was married and had small children. We began four-wheeling across the desert hills. The guide, with the girlfriend sitting on his lap, sat in the passenger seat while I perched on the bunk in the back. Since the van is not 4WD, this cross country trip was somewhat bumpy. It was completely dark by now, and the sand track dipped and disappeared over humps and into dry creek beds. It skirted thorn bushes and crunched over small cactus and dry grass clumps. This was not my idea of a road to a campsite, but Steve seemed committed to see this adventure through. We were hardly in a position to discuss it in detail as the guide spoke English and would understand everything we said. We made no audible comments about his questionable archeological discovery, his acquisition of a girlfriend or the jolting drive through the outback in the dark. After several kilometers of desert driving, we arrived at a flattened area that had obviously been a camp spot for the excavators of *Pampagrande*. It was obviously abandoned because it was littered with trash and dismantled shacks.

The guide assured us he was giving us "permission" to camp here and view the ruins the next morning. He claimed to have that authority and would also notify the local rangers of our presence. He then asked for a tip for the service of bringing us here and after receiving it, disappeared with his girlfriend into the darkness. Steve was delighted with the site as it offered peace and quiet, a view of a few lights twinkling in the village below, and the whispering of the desert breeze. The more remote the site, the better it was as far as he was concerned. The place gave me the creeps. The circumstances by which we came to be here were equally questionable. But, here we were, tired and hungry, and once again, we made the best of it.

We settled in and prepared dinner. Halfway through our simple meal, I heard the "crunch, crunch" of footsteps on the surrounding sand.

"We are about to have company." I said. I was more than right. Just as Steve was gathering his huge torque wrench to use as a weapon, and reviewing his karate moves, it became apparent that we were having company from all sides. From every compass point, out of the desert night came eleven men. They appeared over the tops of small hillocks, circled around the bushes and rushed into the flat area of our camp.

In my mind, I reviewed how to say "Take everything, just let us go." in Spanish.

"Just be cool. Try to act friendly. Let me do the talking." Was about all Steve got out before the men were upon us.

With forced cheerfulness, we welcomed them to our camp. The leader wore a black knit cap pulled down to reveal just his face, a black sweater, army fatigue pants, black boots and carried a rifle. The others appeared to be farmers of varying shapes and sizes, one of which also carried a rifle. The others all carried clubs or hoe handles.

"Who are you and why are you here?" asked the leader.

In our best Spanish we assured him we were tourists and had "permission" from our archeologist-guide to camp here. Of course, pronouncing his name was beyond our ability at this point. The leader finally produced his *Policia National* identification, softened his facial expression and proceeded to introduce each member of his quickly gathered "posse". He had seen our van light from the village below, hoped we weren't grave robbers, and had enlisted the help of his neighbors to surround us in case we had negative intentions. Having met us, he was assured we were just stupid, harmless tourists. He gave us his official permission to camp. In return, we offered to share our simple meal with the posse. After politely declining, each member of the group welcomed us in turn, shook hands and quietly disappeared over the dunes to the village below.

Just as the band of eleven disappeared, a bright full moon rose over the mountains and illuminated the ruins around us. Steve and I still discuss this incident. His take is "See, everything turned our alright." My response is "Yes, but what if…."

Our first eight days in Peru had brought us a police escort, an adopted family, illness and recovery, *cumbia* music in the night, and an encounter with an armed band of men in the desert. We could only wonder what adventures might be ahead of us.

> *"Great works are performed, not by strength, but by perseverance."*
>
> Samuel Johnson

Chapter 29

Organization in the Sand

The wind gusted in off the trackless, treeless, grassless desert. Having crossed hundreds of miles of endless sand, rocks and eroded hillsides, it threw itself hard up against the 15 foot high adobe walls of civilization. We were now in the northwestern desert area of Peru.

Chan Chan covered 15 square hectares of this desert in Peru. The ocean crashed on one side and the mountains rose, bare and dry, on the other. This unlikely setting once hosted a culture rich in art, religion and organization.

The organization of the place struck you full in the face, just as the high adobe walls received the force of the wind. In the same terrain where scattered bamboo mat huts now dotted the desolate landscape, a rich and varied culture had flourished. The basis of its success was due to its organization. It contained over 10,000 dwellings, storage sheds, workshops, courtyards, livestock pens, wells, temples and palaces.

The *Chimu* cultural capital was arranged in nine Royal Compounds. Within each, life was organized around the ruler, his officials, religious leaders, tradesmen and artists, and households. Each contributed an integral part of the maintenance of the community. Each royal leader represented an additional outlying area of desert, seacoast or mountain land. Tribute or taxes in the form of food, livestock, minerals or construction materials were brought to the centers. There they were tallied and stored for future distribution for the good of the community.

The leaders in their turn kept peace, made war, or entreated the gods on behalf of those who toiled for them. The system worked for the benefit and survival of all.

The physical environment that was created under this organizational system was equally inspiring. Each Royal Compound was surrounded by high adobe walls with one opening. To increase its already awesome defensibility, the opening was wide enough for only one person at a time to enter and led to a hallway with a series of angled corners. Each corner provided a stopping point for any attempted invasion. It was hard to get out and even harder to get in. Rushing the compound in an attack would have been impossible.

Inside the walls, the respect and loyalty of the community for its leaders was further heightened by the size and grandeur of immense courtyards. The leader was enthroned on an elevated platform. The adobe walls were plastered in deep relief. The decorations of fish, animals or plants reflected the domains of the particular leader. These original motifs were still clearly visible, sheltered from the desert environment by the high walls and ever turning corridors.

Each compound had one or more water source and resources. Dug deep into the sand, springs gurgled up and filled the ponds. The water reflected the passage of the sun and moon through the worshipful lives of the inhabitants. The stone-lined ponds still function today, filled with water, reeds and passing waterfowl.

We thought about the desperate shacks built of reed mats and sticks stuck into the sand that served as housing for modern inhabitants of the area. They were without water, power or services of any kind. The more fortunate had homes made of adobe bricks or cement blocks. In homes built by the sides of the road, the back yard was a desert filled with blowing plastic bags. Families survived on the money earned by changing tires in the searing desert sun. Their lives seemed to have no end point, to be going nowhere. It was merely survival. They were rudderless, adrift in a sea of sand, as loose and empty as the blowing plastic bags. How had these people come to that place of hopelessness from this place of intense organization embodied by the walled cities we were visiting?

After wandering for hours through just one of the nine compounds, we climbed an observation tower. From our perch high above the walls and courtyards, the immensity of the site overwhelmed us. Spreading in every direction were walled cities, each complete within itself. Built in 1300AD, the culture thrived until 11 years of siege by the Incas brought surrender and abandonment in 1471.

Standing there, buffeted by the same timeless desert winds that had blown long ago, we could imagine the sounds of the bustling cities below us, all set against the even more constant and unchanging sound of the surf crashing nearby. The sense of occupying one small dot of time in the timelessness of history was never more real than it was at that moment.

> *"A man's dying is more the survivors'
> affair than his own."*
> Thomas Mann

Chapter 30

Death on a Bus

While staying at a hotel in Peru, we spent some time with a German man and his Peruvian wife and baby. They were in Peru to visit the wife's family who lived in a small mountain town. They told this story of an experience they had while traveling to visit her family. It is revealing of the economy, mindset and experiences that Peruvians lived with on a daily basis. The husband said:

"The older couple was already on the bus when we arrived. We shared small talk and learned that they had just been in Lima for a few days for medical reasons. The wife had surgery and being unhappy in the city, was returning to their mountain home as quickly as the doctors would allow. It was obvious from looking at her that a few more days, or even a week or two in the hospital would have been advantageous. She reclined against the outer wall of the bus, supported by their bags of clothing, enduring the pain of the trip.

"While she slept, her husband told us of the fear that had gripped them as they first became aware of her illness.

From out of nowhere, she had experienced sharp pains, intestinal upsets and other symptoms. Local medicine men and natural herbal remedies had not eliminated the source of the pain. The traveling health clinic only visited their tiny mountain village once a month. The medic was grim following his examination. He suspected surgery would be required. This had been like a death sentence. There was no money for such treatment. It must be performed in Lima, a long and expensive trip, and an experience beyond their comprehension.

"Family members and village friends began to gather small amounts of money, but charity was not a comfortable way of life in the mountains. Generations of inhabitants were cooperative, but self-supporting. The man told how he and his wife had discussed their options, even considering not having the surgery. Their decision was made under pressure as the pain increased and the urgency became obvious. They sold what they could live without. Neighbors, who did not really need the things, bought them. This form of charity was acceptable, the resulting obligations were manageable.

"Their experience in Lima had been stressful. The world there was so different from their village. The medical people operated on another level of communication, often leaving them both out of decisions and discussions. The surgery was performed, leaving the husband sleeping overnight in the waiting area with all their baggage. He finally was able to join his wife in the hospital room, where he stayed, 24 hours a day, unwilling to leave her side. Her state of unconsciousness following the surgery was upsetting. This signaled imminent death in their tiny town.

But the anesthesia wore off, tubes were removed and ultimately her wish to leave was granted.

"The ride home was obvious agony. The road into the mountains was tortuous, rut filled and never ending. It rained constantly. The continuous stops, jolts and jostling by changing passengers increased her discomfort. Then, when it seemed things could be no worse, the bus broke a drive shaft, relegating it to inaction. In the blinding rain, another bus was flagged down, and the now desperately ill woman was moved."

Their fellow Peruvians were unwilling to assist with this process, so our German friend became personally involved. The Peruvians were unsure why the woman was sick and feared catching some serious illness that would result in their own incapacity. They knew too clearly how devastating this would be to their own families.

Our friend continued, "The new bus was far less comfortable and their seats were in the back. The bumps and potholes were exaggerated there. The woman continued her stoic endurance, moaning softly, but keeping her pain to herself. At one point, her husband told how he was sure she was sleeping. At the next stop, near to their home, he found her rest was complete. The trip had been too much and she had not survived to rejoin her family and friends."

As we sat listening to our friend relate this story, we felt the desperation, the ultimate sadness of the ending. We could imagine the sense of loss the husband must have experienced after months of agonizing over the illness, gathering precious funds, the stress of the trip, and then the angst of returning home alone to an empty cottage and an emptier life. The effects of poverty and inability to access services were all too real and struck people at the most basic levels of their lives. It was a matter of life and death.

> *"What we cannot find on earth
> is not worth seeking."*
> Norman Douglas

Chapter 31

Poor Man's Galapagos

You could feel the tension mounting as the crowd on the dock inched forward. The launch was in place, bright orange life jackets padding each seat. Who would sit where? Which were the best seats? Were there enough for everyone? All the instincts learned during a lifetime of bus riding rose to the surface. The people of this South American crowd were used to being crowded and limited and aggressive. We had been learning this lesson, but had not learned it well. We still hung back, acted politely, said "Oh, no, please, you go first." In short, we were getting pushed aside. If the boat filled up, we wouldn't be on it. We would miss our chance to see the islands off the coast of Paracas, Peru, the poor man's Galapagos.

Firmly in control of the crowd, the tour guide raised her clipboard like a weapon. On it were the names of advanced ticket holders. Also listed were a small group from a nearby hotel and the late-comers who had paid on the dock and now crowded forward in anticipation of a seat. The flash in her eyes and the determination in her face caused the crowd to ease back a step or two. They were intimidated by the authority of the written list and the woman who wielded its power.

"Esteban." she said, reading the first entry. That was us. We had long since dropped all of our other first and last names. They were unpronounceable to our Latin American hosts and took too much time and repetition to arrive at even a recognizable facsimile. *"Esteban."* This was the Spanish name for Steve that they could recognize and pronounce. Spread across Central and South America are lists with entries for the family name of *"Esteban".* They must think it strange that our last names so closely resembled first names.

We were happy and relieved to have our name called. This would not be a pushing match after all. We stepped forward and were handed down into the launch. The seats were quickly filled in the order of ticket purchase. The fiberglass boat moved away, leaving the busy port of Paracas behind. We were headed for *Islas Ballestas,* the poor man's Galapagos, where penguins, seals and sea birds lived, oblivious to their status as second best attractions.

The real Galapagos Islands had eluded us. They were inaccessible due to inflated prices and an oil spill that left the islands in a state of protectionist panic. The *Ballestas* Islands lay off the coast of Peru near the fishing village of Paracas. Prices for a guided tour fit our budget nicely. The real Galapagos would have to wait for some cash-rich future.

On the way to the islands, the speed boat passed curious sea lions that obligingly waved us on our way with shiny black flippers. Sea gulls and pelicans flew overhead, and then nose-dived into the blue-green water, chasing some unseen, but inviting fish.

The rocky islands came into view about 40 minutes from shore. The distinctly layered red, black and gray outcroppings were the result of some ancient uplift of an undersea plate edge. Infill of sandstone had been washed away and the resulting islands were honeycombed with caves, arches, undercuts and grottos.

The cold waters of the Humbolt Current up welled around these islands. You wouldn't think cold water was the favored home of microscopic ocean creatures, but nature has a way of fooling you. The water was filled with nutrient rich plankton and krill. The result was a rest and refueling station for migrating birds from all over the Americas and a breeding site for sea lions. The presence of sea lion pups by the hundreds attracted Orcas and sharks. The giant whales migrating up the coast of South America strained the rich waters, gorged on krill, and enjoyed snacking on the swimming schools of small fish that hovered near the islands.

The rocky outcroppings and ledges sheltered cormorants, terns, Peruvian boobies, pelicans, seagulls and even penguins. The chill waters and abundant fish reminded the penguins of their home far to the south in Antarctica. They stood, upright and slightly aloof from the flying species. They looked civilized and sophisticated in their gray and white tuxedos. Gulls and terns hugged the smallest ledge. They perched on the edge, placing themselves between their fluffy babies and a sudden plunge into the icy water below. Had the flightless babies fallen into the water, they would have become dinner for some other species. Darwin's survival of the fittest was in action here.

The sea lion beaches were equally prolific. Before they came into view, the barking and squeaking gave their presence away. The number of animals that covered the rocky beaches was unexpected. The narrow beaches were filled from wave edge to rock walls by a seething, shifting mass of sea lions. Huge males with thick manes defended their territory and their mates. Their roars and bellows warned off other males. Crossing an imagined boundary line initiated a swift charge by a powerful body and swift bites to the neck and chest of the offender.

Female sea lions lounged in the sun, content to let the males expend energy on imagined infringement of territory. Their job was done. They had bred and now all they had to do was eat, rest and wait for delivery time. The rest of the beach swarmed with shiny, black, squirmy pups from the previous season's breeding. Dozens of pups scrambled out of harm's way every time a male bellowed and charged. The size difference was so great that the very pups the males were defending could easily be crushed by their possessive charge to defend them.

Groups of 30 or 40 pups edged forward to the water's edge, then rushed back en masse as the waves broke on the beach. The less agile were rolled and tumbled as the waves caught them. The least lucky were targets for Orca charges or sharks in search of an easy meal. The squeaking and crying of the masses of pups filled the ear like shrill background music, accented by the deep bellows of the males and the barking calls of the mothers. It was a sea lion symphony of life.

Poor Man's Galapagos

Played out here on these tiny islands was the food chain in action. Plankton and krill were the food for large whales and small fish. Small fish fed the seals and the birds. The seals and birds fed species of whales and larger species of birds. Babies were born, and were killed; they lived to hunt and died to become food. The drama of life and death was persuasive and swirled about the islands like waves.

Weaving in and out among the rocky islands, our boat bobbed in the surge, then pushed forward, past overhanging cliffs and caverns that each wave filled with water and emptied with each ebb. The receding water revealed rocks crusted with muscles, barnacles, sea stars, starfish and urchins. The thickness of this encrustation was further testimony to the richness of the food supply in the waters surrounding these rocky islands. As part of the food chain, the crustaceans fed off the nutrient rich water and then became food themselves.

As we passed through *"El Paseo"*, a giant archway between two parts of an island, we were bade good-bye by the chorus of sea lions, the shrill calls of the flocks of sea birds that dipped and wheeled overhead, and by the sound of the surf as it crashed on the life-filled islands around us. *Ballestas* Islands were a poor man's Galapagos filled with the rich interplay of an active and flourishing food chain and eco system.

> *"Tis distance lends enchantment to the view, and robes the mountain in its azure hue."*
>
> Thomas Campbell

Chapter 32

Where Condors Soar

Is it a bird? A puma? Or a *caiman*? Machu Picchu, the ancient sacred city of the Incas has inspired thousands of questions since its discovery by Hiram Bingham in 1911. The meaning of its design was just one of the questions.

Stepping through the stone city gate, the most famous city of the Incan world spread out below, clinging to the mountain top. At first glance, it was an assemblage of terraces, storehouses, temples and residences. It is obvious there was a plan. But what was it?

Researchers knew the Incas laid out their cities with intricate designs. The resulting cities and temple sites reflected many life forms. The upper part of the city of Machu Picchu appeared to be clinging to the mountain slope like a giant, sunning *caiman*, a reptile closely resembling an alligator.

Facing the city was a sheer conical mountain. It rose straight up from the Urubamba River below. There, on the mountain, watching over the city, and its enemy the *caiman*, was the face of a puma. It was eerie and mystical to be a part of this ancient face-off that was suggested by rock faces, caves and bare spots on the cliff. As you imagined it being contemplated by generations of Inca inhabitants, you began to wonder. Was it a coincidence of nature that this shape appeared in the mountain and city below, or careful planning by Inca architects?

The far side of the city was shrouded in the clouds. Here farmers had lived and tended terraced fields. The fields shaped themselves around the mountain like another puma. Its head was held high, legs stretched toward the river rushing far below. The terraces where crops were grown were so steep that from the top, the terraces immediately below were unseen. The breathtaking and hair raising view of the river below must have distracted many Inca farmers as they bent over quinoa, corn and vegetables. And all the while, the puma's eyes watched from the mountain above.

The mysteries of Machu Picchu didn't end with its shapes. Why was it built in such an inaccessible spot? Protection from attack by other tribes was a motivation. The Incas were annoyed by aggression from Amazonian tribes, but danger to the mighty empire was minimal. Was it protection from the Spanish that motivated them or rumors of the power of the Spanish? The timing of its construction is uncertain, but since guesses of its dating fail to coordinate with the efforts of the Conquistadors to strip the empire of its gold and power, it is doubtful that Machu Picchu was built to resist a Spanish invasion.

Was it a sanctuary for the Virgins of the Sun Temple? The isolated location and self-supporting structure of the economy encourage this idea. The presence of over 1000 inhabitants and unchanging human nature challenge this.

There were too many people and too much interaction for the site to be a sanctuary. So the mystery remains unsolved.

The Incas believed their lives and buildings on earth were reflected by a parallel existence in the stars. They built their cities below constellations, in the shape of animals they saw in the stars and on earth. They laid out their lives in relation to the movement of the sun, moon and stars. Even shafts of light fell in special grooves in sacred rocks in special places within their temples and cities. Shadows marked the seasons. Indications of the equinoxes marked the construction of every building of significance. But why was Machu Picchu here, and in this shape?

A vantage point overlooking Machu Picchu is perched high on the sacred mountain of Huayna Picchu. Steve climbed it, clinging to the sheer rock wall, step after stone step. He squeezed through the cave-like opening at the top. There, spread across the mountain-top in its entirety, lay an answer. The city appeared not like a puma or a *caiman*, but like a giant bird in flight.

Like the condors that sailed through the valley below them, the city sailed under the coordinating stars in the Milky Way above. As designed by Inca architects, it pointed its people along the path of stars, the path of time, toward their concept of the Absolute. All things within it, from its shape, to its shadows, pointed toward that end. The people living within its walls and sheer drop-off cliffs were poised to enter another dimension with every step they took.

Our visit to Machu Picchu raised more than just the hair on our arms and our blood pressure. It raised our respect for Incan ingenuity, engineering and sense of the eternal. The city had water resources and self-contained food production. It sustained itself in a place nature had designed more for the birds than for man. Its use of fitted stones in the construction of temples still defies explanation. Without metal tools, the live stone was worked to form the foundations. Tight joints, interlocked and earthquake proof stone walls, all canted at precise angles, are still not reproducible with modern tools.

The sense of the eternal surrounds you while wandering from terrace to temple. All was in order, designed and incorporated into a larger view of the universe. Shadows fell into grooves and still marked the passage of the sun. Seats in the temple were still lit by the sunrise, marking feast days that are long forgotten, its celebrants long dead or vanished.

Condors still soar over the mountain top and dip into the deep valleys. The sun rises, the stars trace tracks across the night sky. Machu Picchu sits where condors soar, silent testimony to the presence and to the passing of the Incas.

> *"Do not dwell in the past, do not dream of the future, concentrate the mind on the present moment."*
> Sidhartha Gautama, Buddha

Chapter 33

Taking a Break from the Van

I was sitting in Ariquipa, Peru, in a 300-year old stone building with vaulted stone ceilings and archways that were now fitted with glass doors, looking out onto a bustling street filled with cars, taxis, mini buses and pedestrians, all scrambling for their place in the cobblestone streets, and working on a Japanese computer as I typed out email! What an ironic setting.

We had taken the plane back to Ariquipa from Cusco, the jumping off place for visits to Machu Picchu. The flight out of the Andes took 30 minutes. If we had taken the train, we would have been 12 hours to Puno, an overnight stay in a hostel in Puno and then another 12 hours by train back to Ariquipa. The price for the trip by train would have been the same as the price to fly. Since we had gone to Puno (Lake Titicaca) and Cusco (Machu Picchu) by bus and train, we decided to take the quick way back and flew. The flight was bumpy. You flew over mountains, and then foothills, then deserts, all covered with patchy clouds. The up and down drafts from the geographical features lifted and dropped the plane continually. Not being a great flier, I was terrified during most of the flight. Even looking out the window at the dramatically changing terrain below did not help to ease my anxiety. I kept having flashes of scenes from books and movies where planes crash in the Andes (those mountains below us) and the people who survive end up eating one another before they are rescued. But no mishaps occurred and we arrived safe and uneaten.

On our last day in Cusco, we had taken the Sacred Valley Tour. This tour visited two market towns and three ruins in a valley that has been farmed since before written history. Most of the river bottom and the hill and mountain sides were terraced, some by the Incas. The ancient terraces were still in use, producing potatoes (500 varieties), corn, maize, quinoa (a grain like rice) and wheat. In June, the "winter" months, they still freeze-dried the potatoes in the ancient way, spreading them out on the ground, letting them freeze at night, then melt and dry out in the sun during the day. It really worked, although the dry potatoes were weird, like sponges, and when reconstituted, they were spongy and felt funny in the mouth. It was an effective way to preserve food when there was no technology. The small plots that covered the valley, hills and mountainsides were all worked by hand by family groups with tools made of wood. I thought this was strange until we visited a farm family. After the visit I understood that man was the most versatile tool of all. The plots of land were all enclosed by stone fences, or were on such a steep slope that no tractor could ever get to the fields. Plow animals could not climb the slopes or turn around in the narrow terraced fields. That left man to work the soil by hand.

The methods used on these hillsides were a green farmer's dream. Everything pulled or trimmed or left over was composted and the soil stayed rich. It had worked for them for centuries and no changes were in sight. The farm family that we visited was a unique experience. They lived in a small compound, built around a stone lined courtyard. Everything was made of adobe which means these were real mud houses. There was no glass in the windows, and no heat of any kind in the houses. The beds were simply piles of plant material stacked on platforms made of adobe. The cooking was done in the open courtyard over a fire made of small scraps of wood, animal dung and whatever else could be scavenged that might burn. Remember we were at altitude so as a result, it was cold. We were wearing everything we owned and were freezing. The native people who lived on this farm were barelegged and barefooted. We were all so thankful for everything we had, shoes included.

Our visit to the farm included a chance to see firsthand the small adobe hutches for the *cuy,* or guinea pigs that served as a meat source. They were raised near the house and when a special occasion came along or guests were expected, off with their heads. Actually, they kept the heads on. The cooked *cuy* looked up at you from the platter, skinned and fried whole. Tastes like chicken, really. It was a delicacy in the cities and of course, Steve planned on tasting it as soon as we returned to Cusco. He did sample some of the freeze dried potatoes dipped into a sauce they made using the local soil. Rich in minerals, the mud served as a vitamin supplement to their diet.

The life of these people was hard and it showed in their faces and their stature. They were wrinkled and bent. The weather was biting cold and their houses had no heat. They worked hard in the fields to sustain themselves. They had meager possessions but were generous to their guests.

Their wrinkles were from smiling and squinting in the sun. They loved their children and everyone slept together to keep warm in their adobe houses. While their lifetimes were short, and their futures bleak by our standards, they appeared to have been content with life as it had been lived for thousands of years.

The cities and temples in the Sacred Valley were built on the sides of mountains. The stone steps that led to them were a challenge considering the altitude. Those of us who came from the coast, with zero altitude, were not used to the thin air at 13,000 feet. We huffed and puffed our way up the hills. Any thoughts we might have had about being in shape were quickly discarded. Some of the paths skirted the side of the mountain. The paths were only as wide as a foot path and set on such a steep slope that you could not see the ground drop away below the path. My not-so-subtle fear of heights and sharp drop-offs was in full force. But believe it or not, there was not a single missed step or stumble. I saved that for when we got back to the city of Cusco. There I slipped in the freshly washed and slightly muddy cobblestone street and went all the way down onto my backside. I am not sure if my tears were from hurt or from humiliation. I am thankful it did not happen on the side of some mountain.

The Inca structures were built out of cut stone and fitted together like gloves on a hand. The stones were so well matched that not even a piece of paper could be slipped between the stones. However, the houses for the priests and astrologers that lived at the sites were just stone held together with mud-mortar. They only used the cut stones for temples and important places, not housing. All the sites were laid out with plans and purposes. Most were in the shapes of sacred animals: llama, condor, puma, etc. This took planning. Even the fields in some places were shaped like huge trees, or reflected the lines where the sun shown during the solstices. These people were deliberate and in no hurry. Their temples and fields were built to last. And they have lasted long after the inhabitants have vanished.

The markets were interesting. Many of the handcrafts were reproduced en mass somewhere in cottage factories. You saw the same items in every stall in every market. There were some items that were completely original. Steve bought a complete outfit; shirt, pants, hat, gloves, socks, and coca leaf bag. When we arrive back to the United States, he planned to have his usual post-trip dinner. I think everyone will enjoy laughing at his costumes the most!

From here in Ariquipa, we traveled south to the border with Chile and crossed over. We were looking forward to more verdant nature and national parks in Chile after all the cities and deserts in Peru. Hopefully the rumors of bridges being out due to the rain would just be rumors. We stopped by the tourist info offices in Ariquipa and since they weren't really sure where Chile was, we are skeptical as to the quality of their information.

It had been nice to take a break from the van and travel by bus, train, plane and chauffeured tour van instead. But the break was short and we would soon be on the road again.

> *"Security is mostly a superstition."*
> Helen Keller

Chapter 34

The Skin of the Atacama

The skin of the Atacama Desert stretches from horizon to horizon, losing itself in the undulating hills in the far distance. Sharp and white, brittle mineral bones poked up through the brown surface. The body of this stretch of Chile was covered in shifting tan sand.

My initial reaction upon seeing the desert splayed out below us was "Great. Another endless road where you could disappear and no one will ever find you, let alone know that you were lost." Putting that negative thought behind me, I tried desperately to see the beauty of the place. Steve thought the desert was great. He liked the endless miles of nothing and no one. I guess that takes a special person to appreciate. I was not feeling too special about the place when I first viewed it from the mountain pass in Peru. I began to think of it as a living thing as we drove further and further into the rolling sand hills, the sharp, jutting mountain peaks and the rough crystalline chemical plains. It began to take on a personality, a certain sensuality. It was

Two, If By Van
Karen McGinnis

that, or I had begun to hallucinate in the desert heat and emptiness.

The skin of the Atacama was the sand, the finely ground rocks, the sifted surface that cover almost 1500 miles of Chile from the border with Peru to the capital of Santiago. One third of the country's length was covered by this rainless region. The bones of the Atacama were its minerals. Rich in nitrates, copper and iron, the mining products of the Atacama formed the backbone, the economic support of this thin sliver of a country.

Across the sun baked-skin of the desert ran a strip of black and gray, accented with white tape. So obviously man-made, so out of place in this barren expanse of nothingness, racing uninhibited across the desert, the Pan-American Highway stretched from horizon to horizon, running seamlessly beyond the imagination. It seemed to be coming out of nowhere. I soon forgot all the people and places that lay behind us. In this open, sandy void, there was nothing else. All other forms of life ceased to exit in the midst of this powerful desert. Ahead, we knew what awaited us. The Mad Max movies could have been shot here and the endless desolation, the feeling of lonely hopelessness expressed in those movies would have been all the more real for the location choice.

Sitting in the van, feeling the wind flashing hot across your face and knowing that your whole world existed only within your mind and this fragile moving sanctuary, made the intensity of the experience even deeper. The movement of the van meant life here, a cooling effect of breeze on your sweat-dampened skin. Stopping or breaking down meant certain discomfort or worse. Keep moving, keep going forward, ahead must be something more, someone, some change. Once again, the heat got to me and I connected this experience to any other time in my past when just "getting through it" was all that made the trauma bearable. I was not enjoying the Atacama.

The pavement sat on top of a levee of sand. Rolling along its surface, the feeling of being apart from the reality of the desert struck you constantly. The pavement was elevated above the sand, and as further prevention against interaction and intermingling with drifts, there were grooves made by bulldozers which lined the road like corrugations of cardboard. Monotonous dips and ridges ran at right angles to the solid reality of asphalt. The continuous tuck and roll of the sandy surface was like folds of skin left behind by some crazed plastic surgeon. Beyond their fluted edges, the natural form of the desert began and ran on and on to the horizon.

The underlying riches of the region occasionally crept to the surface, festering up like long buried splinters. The mineral salts leached up, grew on the rocks and formed striking crystals. They glittered in the relentless sun, looking like miles of bleached exposed chemical bones. Other types of mineral crystals formed globs and then bunched together, like rocks gone insane. The bulbous, erratic formations stretched to the horizon, a chemical nightmare. Was this the surface of our planet? It bore no resemblance to the gentle green fields of productive crop lands that I associated with home and comfort.

Walking through these fields of chemically created rocks was impossible. They stuck to one another, creating an endlessly uneven and changing surface. They resisted being moved or crushed and the surface was sharp. The huge plains resembled giant pieces of sandpaper, created in the highest grit imaginable. The abrasive surface could sand down a mountain, or skin the leg of a hiker right down to the bone.

From our campground in the Tamarugal National Reserve, we ventured into this saline moonscape. The blobs and mounds and crusts of mineral salts lay gray beneath our feet. There was no grass, no weeds, and no bushes. Occasional trees, the tamarugals, poked up through the crust, always covered with thorns and rough abrasive bark. Holes broken through the crust by previous hikers or cattle yawned black and foreboding. They revealed more salt structures inches below the surface. There was no soil here, just sand and salt and minerals and sun and scrubby trees.

Trying to maintain a hiking rhythm on this irregular surface was comical. The surface was unpredictable. The typical pattern of one step, then another did not work. Each step had to be carefully placed or you would fall through the crust into the holes, or step on a sharp jagged crystal or turn your ankle on a rounded chemical blob. This was not the place to fall to the ground from clumsiness. Sure injury awaited the careless walker. We looked like drunken moonwalkers without the advantage of low gravity to smooth our passage.

Scattered across this giant rocky sandbox of brown skin were scars. The scars are slashes in the surface, created by man. Huge bulldozers cut through the thin skin to reveal layers of sand and ground rock to reach the minerals below. Gleaming white like bones, the rich under-layer of chemical deposits were scraped up, dumped into trucks the size of houses, then driven off across the scarred landscape. The scrapings were then sifted and purified in plants that belched exhaust into the clear, rainless air of the desert. The air would have been clear if it were not for these processing centers. Smog lay like a pall over the endlessly still desert. Instead of vast vistas, the distance was hidden behind the particle-filled air. A high price was paid to retrieve these chemical riches from the soil. The landscape was scarred by the mines and the air was destroyed by the refining process.

Desperate, dusty towns were built by mining companies and sat like scabs on the desert. Here families of laborers and management waited out their assignments. Some assignments lasted a long, rainless lifetime. Life in these towns seemed depressed. It was too hot to venture far in the daytime. At night the sky must have been filled with brilliant stars, but the dust from the refineries obscured the view. Everything was covered in a dusty depressing gray film. Green plants, nurtured by some hopeful resident in a dry dusty yard, soon become covered with the ever-present powder and took on a sad and struggling appearance. I could only imagine what the alcoholism and suicide rate were in a place that offered obscure beauty, no respite from the elements and no view to the outside world.

The seamless skin of the desert rolled up over the sensuous hills to the east and west. Their rounded forms reclined on the desert floor, clothed in shades of rust, red, gray-green and cream. Their smooth shapes were testimony of their agelessness. Ancient rains, wind, blowing dust and even, prehistoric oceans had passed across their surfaces, smoothing, rounding and leaving them behind to bake in the sun. Tattooed with geoglyphs, ancient traders marked their sides, encouraging future travelers to persevere.

Two, If By Van

Karen McGinnis

Someone had been here before. Keep on moving and you too would come to the end of this trackless space.

Man had left his mark on the desert. After their passing from this life, men lay in graveyards of iron crosses and fencing. Slowly, even these elements were reclaimed by the environment as the salts, sand and wind worked on diminishing the markers. Ancient man marked the hillsides. Modern man's marks were mining scars, ghost towns and haze-filled horizons. Beneath it all, the skin of the Atacama stretched on, covering its bones, dominant, ageless and eternal.

> *"Every instant of time is a pinprick of eternity."*
> Marcus Aurelius

Chapter 35

The Smell of Time

It caught you by surprise. The effect was unmistakable. The hair on your arms stood up, your chest tightened, and there was an unavoidable urge to look over your shoulder. It was the smell of time, that certain dense mustiness that you encountered while experiencing the culture, ruins, even the hostels of Latin America.

I first recognized the smell and its implications when I turned my head to the wall of the hostel in Colca Canyon, Peru. It was an old adobe building, built of the red earth found in the region. It had been a hotel or hostel or inn for uncounted years, hundreds to be sure. The walls were close to a foot thick, constructed by hand of the sun-dried bricks that still form the houses most people in the area live in today. The uneven walls were plastered over with more of the same red mud. The uneven, hand finished walls were then painted, perhaps dozens of times, with varying forms of whitewash. The former dirt floor was now covered with a "new" wood floor, perhaps only a hundred years old. Its unevenness added to the charm of the structure and made walking in bare feet an interesting textural experience.

Searching for sleep, I had turned my head toward the wall, and there it was, that hair-raising, dense smell. It was so familiar. Where had I smelled it before? There were many answers to that question. Most recently, it occurred at Paracus, Peru where rooms were filled with ancient textiles, trepanned skulls, and mummies forever frozen in the fetal position as they encountered life after death. The presence of the smell there was intense. It filled the air with the life of another culture, another time, another belief system.

That hair-raising smell was found in the abandoned mining town of Humberstone, now brought to life in a *novela* for Chilian television. The long-gone people are alive again in the imaginations of a romance-hungry population, glued to the screen each evening. While televisions hummed warmly, the reality of the abandoned mining town sat in the Atacama Desert, the wind whistling songs of lives gone by and desires now cold and abandoned.

The smell of time hit you in the face as you peered into caves in the *Valle del Encanto*. Inside the caves and on the surrounding rocks, glyphs tried to tell the story of the prehistoric people who camped there, ground food on those rocks and sipped water from the seeping springs of the valley. You imagined their thoughts as they snared the abundant rabbits, gathered the grains and cactus fruit, and prepared to face the struggles of crossing the desert that lay just beyond the valley walls.

The smell of time was really the remnants of the lives that people had lived in these ancient places. The old smoke on

The Smell of Time

the stone or adobe walls gave off its own perfume. The adobe and wood and stone were all aging and degenerating, giving off gases characteristic of this process. The castoffs of human life, long since thrown away, were breaking down into dust and memories. Together, the perfume, the gases, the dust of the past created a smell that can only be called the smell of time. It was a reminder of the lives filled with struggle and success that passed before us, bringing us a richer present.

> "*The best things in travel are all undesigned, and perhaps even undeserved.*"
> H.M. Tomlinson

Chapter 36

Memories of Tastes and Smells

The influence of German settlers on Southern Chile reflected on the lakes in chalet-style architecture and echoed off the volcanoes like a yodel. We began to sense this influence in the lakeside town of *Villarrica*. Clipped gable houses nestled among the evergreens and bright golden poplars. Dutch Gambrels were decorated with shaped shingles and flower boxes celebrated the sunny days with bright red geraniums. All was typically European. What had happened to the stick houses with dirt floors and thatched roofs? Where were the adobe bricks and decorative iron rebar that was so common in Central America.? Were we still in Latin America, or had some time-space warp happened during the previous night? Only the language remained to remind us of our South American location.

A bakery called Brothaus-*La Casa del Pan* (House of Bread) brought me as close to my grandmother's immigrant baking as I have ever come. Her legendary "butter ring" pastry was proudly displayed on the countertops. This treat of sour cream yeast dough and ground nuts and cinnamon was packed full of memories. It was doled out in my family as a birthday or Christmas treat. It was almost worth having a birthday just to receive one as a gift. The Brothaus version came very close to meeting her high standards for melt-in-your-mouth richness.

We stocked up. You never knew when you might next come upon a bakery. Sometimes the craving for something sweet was so powerful that you frantically scavenged through the van cupboards, searching desperately for anything that resembled dessert. Steve, being the controlled and practical one, resorted to hiding treats in order to preserve them from my rampages. Finding a bakery of this caliber was like suddenly being told it was Christmas, and guess what, you were getting presents!

The next bastion of Germanic influence was *Fruitillar* on the shores of *Lago Llanquihue.* Here bright cosmos blossoms peeked through the picket fences, and mounds of English daisies lined the crushed gravel paths. Shingles, shaped and artfully applied, covered substantial country farm houses. Around them privet hedges and rose gardens created a fairy-tale setting. Lace curtains dangled in every bay and dormer window. Gone were the agaves, the weed fields, and the trash. Dogs were on leashes, not on their last legs.

Buildings dating from the 1800´s reflected the long and prosperous history of the immigrants to this area. Architectural styles included Victorians frosted with gingerbread, Tudors, cottages and peaked roof houses of every style and size. Behind them all, the lake, mountain and volcano views were expansive. We had been transported into a fairy land. More correctly, the immigrants who had settled here had transplanted their sense of style and sensibilities to this new location.

Memories of Tastes and Smells

The only fly in the ointment of this European-style paradise was the temperature. It was cold. Mornings brought a frosty view through fogged van windows. Layers of snuggly sleeping bags became a necessity. This was the price to be paid for the view of snow covered volcanoes and crystal clear mountain streams.

After a walk in the brisk evening air of *Fruitillar*, we were more than ready for a hot meal. We followed our noses, searching for a German treat for dinner. The dining room of the Aleman Club welcomed us with knotty pine paneling and hand crocheted lace curtains.

We were delightfully surprised by our meal. The "special" was the creation of a chef that was either bored, creative, or had a wry sense of humor. On our plates, half a roasted duck reclined on a bed of shredded red cabbage. On the side, round puffed potato "eggs" completed the presentation. Steve and I had a lively debate as to what the side bowl of seasoned applesauce represented. It was just too easy for our imaginations to run amuck.

As we enjoyed our creative meal, a full, golden moon rose through the pink-tinted sunset sky. *Volcán Orsorno* stood majestically to the side, snow capped and cone shaped, the perfect volcano. The whole scene, moon, volcano and sunset sky was reflected in the still waters of the lake. It was a picture postcard. In fact, we found the exact picture postcard the next day at the local museum. This must be the type of scenery local residents enjoyed on a regular basis. We were lucky to have seen it firsthand.

The next morning, as we rolled along a winding country road through rolling fields inhabited by dairy herds and bordered by evergreens and golden poplars shimmering in the fall breeze, we felt a tinge of homesickness. It was for some far off homeland of our ancestors where snow falls, and butter-rich pastries and roasted barn fowl are served in a cozy kitchen warmed by a wood fire. That nostalgia ran blood-deep and was stirred by our visit to the lake district of Southern Chile. Even as we felt that pit-of-the-stomach ache for things past, we realized that this moment would soon become the nostalgia of the future.

> "*Thoughts come clearly while one walks.*"
> Thomas Mann

Chapter 37

A Visit to the Lake Country

The lake country was beautiful. Poplar trees were just turning bright yellow. A tree particular to this area of Chile called the *arucania* had a knobby trunk about 60 feet tall with an umbrella shaped bunch of branches on the top that resembled monkey pod or Norfolk pine. They were evergreen. Some of these trees were thought to be 1000 years old or older. Whole forests of them stuck up into the sky with bamboo and fuchsias growing underneath. Both the bamboo and the fuchsia were said to be native to this part of Chile. I was suspicious. I thought everything originated in the state of California. Well, chalk that up to the learning process. California was not the center of the universe after all.

We took an interesting hike through one of these forests to a waterfall that was coming straight out of the rock. No stream dumped the water. Melting snow water flowed through the volcanic strata straight out into a beautiful cascade over moss covered rocks and tree trunks. It was no trickle. A great rushing waterfall suddenly appeared out of nowhere. The whole thing was surrounded by fuchsias and bamboo and overshadowed by these great tall trees.

There were many small lakes here, tucked into deep valleys. Steve has purchased a used kayak and gear with which to enjoy the abundance of lakes in this area. It was the perfect place for that sport. So our little yellow VW van now had a faded pink kayak strapped to the top along with the "rocket box" storage unit and "Snoopy as the Red Baron" flying on the roof rack. Snoopy started out white and by now was completely black with road grime and soot. We can't decide if we should wash him and put him back on the roof or just let him "ride" until the trip was over to really show the effect of the miles.

After being together constantly for months, Steve decided to take a little "alone time" and do the second part of a two day hike to a *"refugio"* near *Lago Tinquilco* on his own. I went down the mountain on the public transport bus and spent the night at a hostel in Pucon rather than stay alone in a cold van in the middle of a dark forest with no hot showers. There were no other campers nearby, as usual. We consistently had missed the tourist season and often had the national parks completely to ourselves. This made for peace and quiet, but also a lack of cultural exchange and companionship.

Instead of staying alone in the van, listening to the night sounds and wishing I was somewhere else, I stayed in a three-person room which I had to myself and enjoyed an all-the-hot-water-you-want shower. But there was no peace and quiet there. A small group of backpackers were partying in the courtyard outside my room into the wee

A Visit to the Lake Country

hours of the morning. I was beginning to rethink the advantages of traveling off-season and off-the-beaten-path.

The hostel was one block off the main street of the tourist town of Pucon, cozy and safe, but not the place you want to be if sleep is what you are looking for. That was the reality of "hostelling." The places meet all your needs, and generally are filled with people under 30 who don't seem to feel any great need for sleep. That night, at 1AM, I got up out of bed and went to the patio outside my room and mentioned that the hostel had a 12AM lights out policy. I am sure that I was that energetic, young and excited about new friends when I was their age and deep in the wilds of some foreign country with my own college buddies. But that night, I just felt old and sleepy.

> *"Toto, I've a feeling we're not in Kansas any more."*
> Noel Langley, 1911
> "The Wizard of Oz"

Chapter 38

Crossing the Continent

The word "Patagonia" conjures up pictures of warm polar fleece jackets in bright colors. Or perhaps even thoughts of wind swept plains where clothes like that might come in handy. Most Californians would stop and think for a minute before venturing a response as to just where in the world Patagonia might be. Asia? Russia? Our cross-continental jog of South America helped us to know just exactly where Patagonia really was and to define it in a whole new set of terms.

Patagonia is more than an area of open, wind swept plains. The southern tip of South America from Buenos Aires to the tip of Cape Horn defines the boundaries of Patagonia. It stretches from the Pacific Ocean to the Atlantic Ocean. More than plains, it is made up of mountain ranges, volcanoes, glaciers, icy lakes and fjords.

The challenge of crossing the Patagonia "from sea to shining sea" presented itself to us when our previously "best laid plans" ended up in the dumper. We had made arrangements to ferry the van and ourselves from *Puerto*

Montt, Chile to *Puerto Natales* further south. Then we would drive on to *Tierra del Fuego*. We all know what happens to best laid plans, they go awry.

Our plans went bad when the engine of the one and only ferry died. Repairs were estimated to require three weeks, then, maybe, there would be service. Three weeks is an eternity when time is of the essence and you still have at least four more big countries to visit. Beside that, winter was approaching and being this close to Antarctica meant it was going to get cold very soon, very, very cold. The passes in the Andes would be closed or even more dangerous to cross than they normally were. We also had to consider that we were staying in our camper-van, not a heated room with hot showers. Sleeping in a van in freezing temperatures presents its own set of challenges. The inside of the van windows become glazed with ice. When the ice melts, the water drips down onto your clothes and bedding. We had become adept at changing clothes while encased in a sleeping bag, but that didn't mean we had come to enjoy it. Waiting for the ferry engine to maybe be fixed and maybe be running was not an option for us.

We formulated Plan B, our second best laid plan. Instead of traveling south by sea, then by land to *Tierra del Fuego*, we would cross Chile, the Andes, then Argentina by land, travel south overland to *Tierra del Fuego,* then pick up the ferry again in *Puerto Natales* for the trip back north. But first, we had to cross the continent from the Pacific to the Atlantic, including the Andes Mountains in between.

Luck was with us and we caught a short, overnight ferry to *Chacabuco* on the Chilean coast. This 24 hour trip saved us about 1000 miles of dirt-road driving and about a week of time.

Packed tight with loaded semi-trucks and a few passenger cars and trucks, the ferry rode deep and smooth in the water. The channel passed between uninhabited islands on the west side and forested mountains topped with snow on the east. A whale spouted. Dolphins raced the ferry, grew bored and left us in their wake. Seals played and birds swooped. The passage was serene and spectacular.

Sleeping on the ferry was impossible. We had sprung for the more expensive seats, they reclined. Well, they sort of reclined. You were still sitting in a position similar to an airline seat. If you were tired enough, sleep would come. Except that the truck drivers who were supposed to be spending the night in the passenger lounge while their trucks were ferried along, had snuck into the higher priced lounge and had assumed the position in any empty chair. No one would have minded their presence except for the fact that they snored. It was obvious which ones were freeloading. They knew the ropes. They waited until the steward passed through the cabin for the last time in the evening, entered and sat down in an empty chair and immediately fell in to a deep and noisy sleep. Nothing would wake them until we docked.

Steve can sleep anywhere, anytime. I am not so lucky. I could not get comfortable. The angle of the reclining seats did not allow for any position except face up, flat on your back. My legs twitched. My back ached. I wanted to scream at the snoring men to shut up and get out. Sleep deprivation hit me hard. Steve did his best to contain my frustration, and spread sleeping bags on the floor in the corner and at sometime during the night, I almost fell asleep. I would be so happy to get back into our cozy van bunk. I guess everything is relative.

After being dumped off the ferry in the dark at *Chacabuco*, we felt our way along the mountain road toward *Coihaique*, the closest town. We felt every seam in the uneven cement road. We felt every broken, dropped section which unexpectedly jolted us on the dark winding road. As soon as we could, we pulled into the driveway of the closed Rio Simpson National Park and settled down for the night. Better and far safer to negotiate this kind of road in the daylight.

Our first order of business come daylight was to find a hose at the park building and wash the ferry's diesel exhaust from our van. Negotiating the cracked cement roads was hard. It became nearly impossible when peering through the one small spot on the grease smeared window that we had rubbed clean the previous night.

We stocked up on food one last time at a store in *Coihaique* and prepared to tackle the mountain pass into Argentina. We had food for a month, new tires and new brakes, full gas cans and a positive attitude. I think we had covered all the essentials.

Heading southeast we began our circuit of huge *Lago General Carrera*. This lake and its sister, *Lago Buenos Aires*, spanned the border between Chile and Argentina. It took us two days to drive around the southern half of the lakes. The road was *ripio*, which is South American for dirt and gravel. It is impossible to travel more than 20 or 30 miles per hour. The surface resembled a ribbed washboard covered in small stones. The whole time you were driving you prayed you wouldn't get a flat tire or run out of gas. We had taken preventative measures and hoped our new tires and extra gas were up to the test.

We seldom saw another vehicle. That alone was unsettling. What were we doing out here? No one else was crazy enough to drive this way. What we did see were herds of sheep, guided along by cowboys or *gauchos* wearing leather chaps, capes, berets and carrying whips. These were their real work clothes, not costumes. Now we were sure we were crazy. We had passed through a time warp and were now in the frontier days of Argentina.

The route was lined with rose bushes. Formerly covered with pale pink or lavender roses, they now were a riot of red rose-hips. With their leaves still green, it looked like Christmas had arrived in April, then gone completely mad over its bad timing. The hills were covered with red and green bushes. The roadsides were lined with them and they reached out to scratch the sides of the passing traffic. Meadows were dotted with mounds of green bushes, thick with the bright red seed pods. Even this colorful celebration of fall, as the seasons are reversed in the southern hemisphere, was soon going to be upstaged.

The first evening on the shores of *Lago General Carrera* brought an explosion of color. Steve had launched his kayak on the crystal clear lake. As he floated like a leaf on the cold glacial water, the gravel bottom looked close enough to touch. Then the sun began to set behind the snow capped mountains to the northwest. The sky lit up to the southeast. Starting high in the sky, the hues ranged from palest blue to pink to purple. Cut sharply by the startling white of the snow capped mountains, there then appeared a dead-stop color change of black granite mountain mass.

As the lake met the mountain bottom, the color exploded again, in reverse. The reflected colors ranged back from darkest blue-black to shocking white to purple, rose and baby blue. The reflection was so perfect, so precise on the still lake surface, it seemed as though someone had sliced through the sky, snow, and mountain, then laid the slice over onto the mirror-like lake. We watched in awe as the colors grew, intensified, and then faded into a star-studded night.

Heading east, we ground along the *ripio* road, interrupted only by cows herded by poncho draped *gauchos*. Hitting the pass in first gear, we struggled past men with boxes of dynamite. The road was so narrow that they were still working on blasting openings in the rock. We crept past, the last vehicle to be allowed through before the blasting began, then high-tailed it for the border, thankful not to have come a day later when the pass would have been blasted closed.

The Chile and Argentine borders were organized and uneventful. We had passed into new terrain. All around us stretched the steppes. Covered in golden mounds of grass and low-growing shrubs, the open, wind-swept plains stretched off into the horizon in every direction. To the east, a few flat topped mesas looked as though they had gotten lost on their way to Arizona and ended up here.

Rheas or *Nandu*, a flightless relative of the ostrich, picked at the golden grass clumps. *Huanaco*, looking like refined llamas, gazed at us as we passed by on the now, nicely paved asphalt road. Cattle and sheep herds moved aimlessly across never ending pastures. The only other moving things to be seen were the pump heads of oil wells. They dotted the landscape and helped pay for the road on which we now zipped across the continent.

One day of driving brought us across the steppes. The scenery can only be described as same-same. Every day we saw the same grasslands, same animals, same wind, same cold. In the distance, the same cloud formations hovered just above the flat landscape, alternately dropping rain and simply sailing along in the wind.

Then suddenly, there it was, the Atlantic Ocean. I was thankful to see it looked very much like an ocean should, blue and with waves. Except of course that to a West Coast girl it was on the wrong side of the continent. Looking at the ocean now meant looking east, not west. It meant looking for a sunrise, not a sunset. It meant looking at gale force off-shore winds that blew the tops right off the breaking waves. No wonder they called the Pacific Ocean "pacific." Compared to this part of the Atlantic, the Pacific was calm and welcoming. Here the Atlantic was angry and cold.

Patagonia, from sea to shining sea. It was a journey by sea and by land. It was filled with color in the bushes, in the changing tree leaves of the passes and in the spectacular sunsets. It was tedious, grinding driving over *ripio* roads, and speedy plains crossings on newly laid asphalt. It was rich in people scenery, from fishermen to cowboys, oil riggers to dynamite handlers. It was long and it was short.

Crossing the continent was many things, all of them beautiful in some unique way.

> *"People who like this sort of thing will find this the sort of thing they like."*
>
> Abraham Lincoln

Chapter 39

Visiting the 50's

Mentioning the 50's makes me think of Ward and June Cleaver, wide tree-lined streets, and those odd-shaped drive-in burger joints. We ran smack-dab into the 50's as we headed south through *Tierra Del Fuego*.

The 50's are alive and well in a small ENAP (Argentina's national oil company) town with the unlikely name of *Cerro Sombrero* (Hat Hill) in the province of *Primavera* (Spring). It sounds like the setting of a second rate novel but these are really the names of real places. In the flesh, it is a breath of fresh air in a complicated modern world.

We drove into *Cerro Sombrero* just at dusk. It sits on the Patagonian *pampa* on the north end of the island of *Tierra Del Fuego*. Even though it was after 5 PM, municipal offices were still open.

"Un sitio de acampar?" we inquired. We needed a place to camp, or at least park our van for the night. Our optimistic inquiry met with an enthusiastic, 50's-style, small town response. Not only was there a brand new, municipal camping and guest area right on the river, but Sergio, a

young public servant from the old school of public service, would guide us there in his car. The fee? Two dollars US for spending the night, use of facilities and electrical hookups. Both the price and the service were a blast from the past.

As Sergio guided us the eight blocks through the entire town, we saw that there was more to *Cerro Sombrero* than just a cluster of houses and maintenance buildings perched on a hill. Built in the 50's by a North American oil company, the architect-designed town resembled Middle America in architecture and facilities. The center of town radiated off the sports complex, church and store.

Remember Quonset huts? Quonset huts were shaped like giant cylinders, cut in half from side to side and laid with the cut side on the ground. The sports complex looked like three giant huts, each with a full wall of glass on each half-circle end, and with a square glass atrium built between the arch shapes to connect them. One hut was the huge indoor pool with high dive. Steve's entry dive brought applause from a group of 10 year-old boys clinging to the side. The opposite hut housed basketball and volleyball, both actively in use. The center span was roofed in glass and covered a garden with walkways, reflecting pools, park benches and full size trees. We discovered that these buildings made such extensive use of glass and were so actively used because the climate in this part of Argentina was heavily influenced by the nearby Antarctic. It was cold and windy. Inside these arches, it was sheltered, warm and inviting. We visited the facility twice, a week apart. Both visits found it in full use by children and adults. Admission: free.

Visiting the 50's

The store, restaurant and theater (also free) featured that boxy 50's design with walls of glass set into modernistic squares and rectangle patterns. The church was a steel beam, A-frame structure, painted pink. With wide sidewalks, grass planting areas around statues and busts of heroes, this place was a movie set for "Back to the Future." The cast of extras on this movie set included gaggles of scurrying children, young couples toddling snow-suited babies, and families out for an evening at the pool and sports complex. After a brisk swim or a rousing game of basketball, a stop at the store for ice cream was in order. I half expected to see Wally and the Beaver among the strolling townspeople.

The attitudes of the residents were even more like the 50's than the boxy pastel houses. Sergio left his desk to guide us through the town. Without having paid a cent or left our name anywhere, we received the key to the buildings at the municipal camp. The local police officer used his walky-talky to find out when the only restaurant opened so we could have a hot meal. The waiter at the restaurant, Nelson, left the restaurant, tapped on our van window and let us know he had arrived and welcomed us in. Even the meal was from the 50's; salmon, American-style mashed potatoes and vegetables. Mom could have made it if she had been cooking in the 50's.

Cerro Sombrero was a warm spot in the cold *pampa* of *Tierra Del Fuego*. It had all the physical charm of a well-preserved lady dressed in the clothes of another era. It had the personal charm of people with warm hearts, old-fashioned trust and welcoming attitudes toward strangers who had entered their little refuge set in the past. This time, the best of things was timeless.

> "The proper use of willpower is not
> conquest and subjugation, but the
> disciplined control of one's own mind"
> Seven Pillars of Enlightenment
> Harry Palmer

Chapter 40

Fire and Ice

The steep granite mountainsides were ablaze. The red, orange and yellow colors flashed down the steep slopes and ended abruptly at the edge of the clear, alpine lakes. The glacial waters reflected back the colors of the surrounding hills. As we wove our way along the mud and gravel road, the flaming trees reached out to us, trying to cross the roadside strips of low mounding grasses. High above, the stark white, snowcapped peaks stretched for the sky. Misty clouds formed, engulfed the mountain tops, then abandoned them as the wind rushed them to new horizons.

The fires of *Tierra del Fuego* in the fall are the changing colors of the leaves on the larch and *lenga* trees. Their summer green turns to bright red, flaming orange and luminescent yellow. All four colors can be present on the same tree. Or a single tree may simply burst into a single color. The variations of colors intermixed with green trees made the rolling foothills and abrupt mountain passes of the island a celebration of hues. Originally named by Hernando Magallanes (Spanish spelling) or Fernando

Magellan in English, in 1520, the real fires of *Tierra del Fuego* were man-made. The *Onas* or Selknam tribe inhabited the island. Apart from a few skins, they wore no clothes and built only brush shelters against the Antarctic winds. They built instead, huge fires to warm themselves. These fires were clearly visible to the men on Magallanes' ships. With bonfires lining the rugged shore, the sailors who struggled against the wind and suffered in its icy grip must have perceived the land as a land of fires, a *tierra del fuego*.

We found the island to be equally a land of ice, a *tierra del hielo*. Winds from the Antarctic whipped the shore. Mountains ringed the harbor off Darwin's Beagle Channel where the world's southernmost city of Ushuaia huddled. Little except snowcapped islands separated it from Cape Horn, that southernmost piece of land that was the bane and often the death of explorers and travelers alike.

In the *Parque Nacional de Tierra Del Fuego*, we took the obligatory picture of ourselves against the "End of the Road" sign. We had officially reached Land's End. The sign advised us that "Here ends the road." Only 17,818 miles separated us from Alaska according to the sign. Since we had driven over 20,000 miles to reach the spot, we assumed they were measuring "as the crow flies" and not as the VW van rolls.

A sunny day allowed us to hike among the brilliant trees, beaver dams and sphagnum moss bogs of the park. Steve off-loaded the kayak and paddled the waters of the Beagle Channel, returning just as the weather changed and an icy rain began to fall. During the night, the rain turned to sleet and the wind blew "stink", hard and strong off the icy sea. The next morning our camp spot at *Bahia Ensenada*, right on the channel, was dressed in a layer of white. Fresh snow had fallen all the way to the water's edge.

We took the layer of white stuff as an omen of things to come and headed north, leaving the land of fire and ice behind us. The trees that had formerly burned in brilliant fire-like colors, now smoldered in a haze of white, their fire subdued by the icy snow.

The end of the road at *Tierra del Fuego* was a goal realized, a milepost found and now left behind. Our trip was not yet at an end. We were still at the bottom of the planet, experiencing fall weather in April and looking winter full in the face. We began looking forward to driving northward, to new adventures on the trip home to sunshine, real coffee, family and friends.

> *"A man travels the world over in search of what he needs and returns home to find it."*
> George Moore

Chapter 41

On the Icy Trail

We left the windy, icy islands of *Tierra Del Fuego* behind and headed north. Across the Strait of Magellan lay the spectacular, but equally windy and icy *Torres del Paine* National Park. On the rocky ground of this dramatic site, Steve and my divergent travel styles would surface.

Steve's travel philosophy is "If I don't need it to survive, I don't need it." Mine is "There's more to life than mere survival." It was inevitable that we would select different paths at some point on the trip.

We reached the separation point at the *Torres del Paine Hosteria* in the national park of the same name. The *hosteria* or hotel was snuggled up against snow-topped mountains. Behind the mountains rose the even taller, spectacular granite towers of pink and gray called the *Torres del Paine*. Many things in this area were named after the explorer who had discovered them, whose last name was Paine.

Two If By Van   Karen McGinnis

To reach the hosteria, we ground along 125 km of dirt and gravel *ripio*. *Puerto Natales* lay behind us to the south and the *torres* beckoned ahead. As soon as we entered the national park, the road disintegrated into a wide dirt track. The road was now a mix of rocks, rain-washed gullies, water-filled and ice topped potholes and blind uphill turns. It crossed glaciated streams without the aid of bridges. It bypassed small waterfalls on platforms of planks. The absence of side rails was unnerving as you looked off one side to the water spilling down the rocks in an icy rush.

Then the road crossed the wide *Rio de Paine*. There was a one lane metal bridge anchored to the land on both sides by steel cables. We came to refer to this bridge as "the bridge of pain."

We approached the bridge with caution. Just past the cables we discovered it was even narrower than we had first thought. Our van would not fit. We were stopped just before the first metal upright of the bridge. In that position, I reached out the open passenger window and unscrewed the side mirror. I had to hold it, still partially attached, as we inched forward across the bridge. We now fit by just inches.

After 7 km of more dirt, potholes, gullies and ruts, we arrived at the foot of the *torres*. The park ranger warned us that the *refugios* and campgrounds might be closed. He was just being nice. Of course they were closed. We were the only campers. There was no water, electricity or facilities in the usual camp spots.

We were forced to accept accommodations at the hotel, for the same price as the rustic, basic *refugio*. (Life can be tough.) The modern hotel was built in a rustic style, but the accommodations and service were first class. The split-log covered buildings spread across the knoll and offered a spectacular view of the valley and mountains all around. Yellow poplars and multi-hued *lengas* colored the grounds. It was surrounded by a working *estancia* or sheep ranch. Real cowboys and shepherds added human color to the hotel grounds. They herded sheep across the lawn, headed for the pastures beyond.

It was a water-colorists dream come true. I was in heaven. Modern facilities, constant and comfortable heat, hot water and beautiful views. Steve was happy, too, but this was way past his "survival" level. He was anxious for something more adventurous.

His first adventure on the site was a six hour hike to the base of the actual granite towers. The trail began at the hotel and hugged the base of the *Almirante Nieto Mountain*. On its side was the Torres Glacier. The *torres* themselves were just beyond.

The clouds hung low. The hike was like walking in a rain cloud. As I enjoyed my warm, quiet refuge, he hiked until long after dark. He returned, wet from head to toe from the rain. Three or four layers of hiking clothes dried in the bathroom as he enjoyed the "non-essential" hot shower.

This kind of hiking was not my idea of a good time. We were in the middle of a mountain range still being shaped by glaciers. There were snowcapped mountains at each of the four compass points. The weather was changeable and potentially dangerous. At least it seemed dangerous to delicate indoor types like me. The wet, muddy ground was either slippery or rock hard with frost. Given all these conditions, it did not seem like ideal hiking terrain or hiking weather.

This was the perfect time for each of us to enjoy nature in our own way. I would remain at the hotel to paint and write and read in comfort. Steve would attack the surrounding terrain by trekking cross country.

But first we had to cross back over the "bridge of pain" to reach the jumping off point for the hike. In order to get Steve there and then make it back to the *hosteria*, I would have to drive the van across the bridge, over the rutted and forbidding roads and then drive back, alone. The first step was driving across the narrow metal bridge. The driver's side mirror served as a guide. If I kept it inches from the steel side rails, the van would just fit. I found out what would happen if your attention wandered for a split second. The result was a van wedged against the steel girder. After a tricky back and forth maneuver with a 20-year old manual stick shift and a little scraped paint on the wheel flair, I freed the van and slowly continued across the bridge. With my nerves shot and the van scraped, I escaped the "bridge of pain." I was so relieved to be over the bridge that once on the other side; I stopped the van, jumped out and stood crying and shaking by the roadside. There are many things in life that test your determination. I had not expected to be tested on a narrow metal bridge in the middle of the glacier country of Argentina. I guess you take your tests when they are given to you and just hope you pass.

A ferry boat ride took Steve across *Lago Pahoe*. There, on the trail, he met three American students on vacation from university classes in Santiago, Chile. This was their first experience at hiking. Together the group of four hiked to a spot near the huge Gray Glacier. Steve helped them set up camp as their tent had gone for a swim when one of the students, Scott, had taken a fall on the muddy ground and encountered nature in an icy creek.

With camp established, it was time for a meal. Scott, Annnise and Amber broke out their cold granola. Steve offered to share his freeze dried Sierra Chicken. "Interesting." was the height of their enthusiasm for this acquired-taste food. They weren't that cold or hungry, yet. With the meal, they shared experiences, or lack of them. Steve told them about hiking in Nepal, Tibet and the California Sierras. They told him about how hiking seemed like a lot of cold, hard work.

After a long, cold night on the boggy ground, Steve was up early and exploring the nearby glacier trails. Upon returning to camp, a thank-you note from the young hikers told of their torturous night and their hope for better, warmer hikes in the future. Steve is still not sure if they packed it in and went home, or continued on up the trail.

Near the glacier, Steve met some carpenters building a new *refugio* for the next tourist season. As a carpenter himself, Steve and the workmen became fast friends. They shared the national drink of friendship, *yerba maté* along with construction and outdoor stories. The *maté* was another of those acquired tastes. The outdoor stories included tales of a puma that was prowling the trails of the glacier.

The second night on the trail was even colder. Without the rainy cloud cover, the temperature dropped and the stars were brilliant. The morning revealed a dusting of frost on everything. Every blade of grass, leaf and mud hole was frozen solid.

The trail, which was filled with wet boggy areas, was now crispy and slick. The horses that carried tourists and supplies had deepened the mud on the trail. The hoof prints filled with water from the spongy ground and now speckled the paths with bright chunks of ice. Hikers trying to avoid the mud, sludge and ice on the path were taking ever wider detours along the sides. Each set of footsteps on the frozen grasses broke down the ground cover and widened the muddy path.

With aluminum walking sticks, hiking boots and experience, Steve attacked the trail. He went down in the threatening conditions and fell squarely on one of his sticks. It was bent and still can't be disassembled. Better a bent walking stick than a broken ankle.

The bright, clear day made the walking go as well as could be hoped. Steve reached the camp for the third night at midday. It was in perpetual shadow from the mountain and trees and showed no sign of thawing any time soon. The thought of spending a cold afternoon and night in this refrigerator was not appealing. Somewhere in the back of his mind, he saw me enjoying the view, paints spread out near the radiator, and an open book nearby. It seemed an inviting alternative to a night on the frozen ground.

Tightening his pack straps, Steve set off to accomplish the next segment of the hike. Could he complete the six hours of trail before dark arrived. Just as dusk was approaching, a sphagnum bog appeared on the trail. Or did the trail disappear into the bog? A wide expanse of cold, muddy, spongy ground was all there was to be seen. The prospects were dim.

Taking his bearings from the mountains, he located what would be the foot of the mountain behind the hotel. Just as the full moon rose, he took off cross-country, leaving the boggy trail behind. A combination of instinct, moon light, good night-vision and the ability to use walking sticks as feelers led him to the river near the hotel. Following it down, he located the bridge. From there, the established trail led quickly to civilization.

I was so surprised to see him in the hotel hallway. I had just come from cooking my dinner in the van and was anticipating another evening of reading and warmth. He was one or two days early, and it was pitch dark outside. Again, he was soaked to the skin, this time from the inside out. The effort to make it back had generated so much sweat that he was steaming.

It was a happy homecoming. I was happy he was back early with only a bent walking stick as damage from the trek. I would find out later about the aching muscles, swollen feet and need for a full day of complete rest. He was happy because he could see the hot shower and warm room that would be his home for the night instead of a cold tent on mucky frozen ground. Our two approaches to appreciating nature were worlds apart, but had left us both satisfied and reunited in the end.

*"To like and dislike the same things,
that is indeed true friendship."*
Sallust 86-35 BC

Chapter 42

Learning to Drink *Maté*

I thought Californians were hooked on coffee until I saw Argentineans and Uruguayans drinking *herba maté*. Building a Starbuck´s in every shopping mall is child's play compared to the lengths these Latin Americans will go to, to access their favorite drink.

Knowledge of *herba maté* as a tea-like beverage hit Europe in 1592. In a written history of the Spanish conquest of South America, a reference to the natives chewing or drinking an infusion of herbs was included. They was thought to give the user higher resistance to fatigue. Some even thought the herbs had magical powers. Today we call these powers the reaction of the body to caffeine and nicotine, two ingredients included on the label of the *herba maté*.

The Spanish writer of the 1592 history also made a mistake about the classification of *herba maté*. It was not an herb at all, but the leaves, stems, and fibers from a holly-like shrub that had been pruned off, dried, toasted and ground. During the days of forced labor, it gave the natives greater energy. Today it provides a stimulating boost to drinkers, and meets many social needs.

Drinking *maté* can create camaraderie and open social doors. While having our muffler welded together for the fourth time, Steve was offered *maté* by the shop owner. Sharing the *amargo* or bitter version of the tea with the shop crew made Steve one of the guys. It led to the shop owner giving us a reference to another friend who had a nautical club and a campground right on the river. We were able to use the facilities on two separate occasions, even though it was off season and they had to leave the doors of the club unlocked all night for us to use the showers. The bond that had been formed over the cup of *maté* was far reaching and had broad benefits. Friends of a *maté* drinking friend became your friends as well.

Steve's second encounter with *maté* was on his hike through *Torres de Paine*. He had met some carpenters in the park who were working to build a refuge for the next season. As they chatted, they shared their *maté* with him. The word "shared" must be taken literally when used together with the *maté* drink. One gourd, cup or calabash of the warm tea is passed around among several drinkers. Each one drinks in turn out of a metal tube with a strainer on the bottom. Sharing this *"bombilla"* and ignoring the potential sharing of germs is part of the ritual. In fact, this makes it an act of *"amistad"* or friendship. If you have been accepted enough to be asked to drink, you will be expected to share without hesitation.

The *maté* the carpenters shared with Steve was also *amargo* or bitter. This version of the drink has a flavor closely resembling stomach bile. It is considered a man's drink and is common among construction workers, mechanics, and *gauchos*. This stereotyping seems acceptable among *maté* drinkers.

After the bitter cup has been passed around the circle two or three times with warm water added as it goes around, the taste either mellows, or one becomes used to the bitterness. You either get used to it, some drug in the drink begins to have an effect on you, or you continue to wince at every sip. If you drop out of the circle, you may loose face and forever join the ranks of "a wimpy tourist who comes from a place where life is soft."

We began to think there might be something to this *maté* drink. Grocery stores had aisles full of the product. It was offered in different flavors, blends and grinds, just like the coffee we missed so much from the states. Shops in every town specialized in *maté* cups, of every description. Some were plain hollow gourds. Some were silver. There were even *maté* cups made from the hooves of cows. We couldn't help but think how that would affect the flavor.

Other equipment for *maté* drinking was available. *Bombillas* or tubes with strainers came in every size and type of material. For the dedicated *maté* drinker, there was a type of stadium bag made of reinforced leather which held the *maté* cup, *bombilla, maté* itself, sugar, and a special thermos to hold the hot water. Everything was handy and carried over the shoulder like a masculine purse, ready to create *maté* at a moments notice. We observed people strolling in parks, driving cars and trucks, sitting at desks in offices, and working at ticket booths. The filled and ready *maté* cup was either at hand or actively being used as they engaged in their daily activities. We were the most amazed at drivers, in the thick of wild traffic, calmly pouring *maté* and sipping it through specially bent *bombilla* that allowed them to keep their eyes on the speeding cars. Talk about drinking and driving.

We took the plunge and purchased a small *maté* set. Curing the *maté* cup takes several days and involves many steps. At the end, your *maté* cup is appropriately grungy with stains from the leaves. The inside of the gourd or wooden cup is flavored with the residue of the *maté* infusion. The curing process does mean that a stinky cup full of ground tea-like leaves is hanging around the kitchen or in our case, the van, for days on end, reminding you of just how, uh, appealing, the resulting drink will be.

We were such novices that our cup barely produced a drinkable product. We tried adding sugar, which made it a *"gringo"* drink, no slam intended. We needed help from a *maté* professional, or a *cebador*.

We found help in *Radatilly*, a beach town in Argentina. A city employee of the tourist bureau invited us to his house after a tour of the fossil-rich hillsides around the town. Daniel and his wife welcomed us to their new, but tiny house. There in the kitchen-dining-living room, we got a real lesson in *maté* drinking. The cup was packed with leaves and only a small area was left open on one side. The hot, not boiling water was carefully poured in to this hole in the leaves. Pouring the water directly on the leaves bruises them and makes the tea bitter. We already knew about the bitter part.

After adding the water, Daniel let it set for a few minutes. Then he took a deep draw on the *bombilla,* and to our

Learning to Drink Maté

surprise, bent over the kitchen sink and spit the whole thing out. We thought it must really taste bad if an experienced drinker like Daniel had to spit it out. Maybe we hadn't been such wimps after all. He explained that this was just part of the ritual and had the effect of eliminating the bitterest part of the drink. Custom demands that the *cebador* or preparer, draw it off and spit it out. It was sort of like sacrificing his taste buds to save those of his friends. I was grateful, but it was not the most charming part of the ritual.

Fortunately things got better after that. We sat around the table, chatting about life and passing the cup. After repeated refilling, the taste improved, and we even began to like it a little. I mentioned that Steve and I both drank our tea and coffee with sugar. Oops! I had revealed that we were wimps, even with tea and coffee. But Daniel was gracious, and showed us how to add sugar to the hole left in the *maté* leaves and then pour the water over the sugar. No stirring allowed.

Conversations led to tea drinking in other cultures. *Maté* met the challenge. Milk was heated in a special pitcher and poured over the *maté* and sugar. We were starting to approach the taste of English tea or even chai. We began to have hope that someday we might be able to actually enjoy *maté* drinking, and quit thinking of it as just a test of manhood.

I began to like the mate ritual even more when Daniel's wife brought out the chocolate covered cookies. "Of course," she said with a smile, "Chocolate is good with everything, even *maté*." She was a woman after my own heart. We learned that adding other ingredients, like lemon, or serving side plates of certain desserts could mean anything from "I want to be your sweetheart." to "Never come back here again."

We realized the ultimate saturation of *maté* into the culture at a gas station. Along the side fence of the modern station were several "service" machines for customers. There, next to the air, water, vacuum, and window washing materials, stood a shining hot water dispenser. It's specially designed spout fit perfectly into a thermos and dispensed water heated to the perfect temperature for *maté*. As we watched, we saw that it was popular with customers, who waited for a turn to fill their ever-present thermos or *maté* cup with the piping hot water.

We no longer thought that *maté* was simply addictive. We now knew that for many Latin Americans it was meeting more than just a physical need. It created a social environment for sharing and getting to know one another and meeting strangers. It created a feeling of trust among those sharing the drink. It was a statement of friendship and communion. We felt lucky to be included as those we met shared a part of their way of life with us.

> *"I traveled a good deal all over the word, and I got along pretty good in all these foreign countries, for I have a theory that it's their country and they got a right to run it like they want to."*
> — Will Rogers

Chapter 43

Virtually Real Driving

Forget everything you know about the rules of the road. Driving courtesies and customs no longer apply. Prepare to test your responses, your intuitions, and your ability to adjust to the unexpected. Enter the world of reality driving, South American style. It's an experience more exciting than any driving video ever made.

The object of your virtually real driving experience is to reach a camp spot in the beach area of the city at which you will spend the night. To reach it you must first survive the traffic. The objective has no address, only a vague reference that it is located on a *punta* or point on the beach road. There are many *puntas*, so you must select the one closest to a street that has a name you recognize. Remember, if you select the wrong *punta*, you must repeat the entire experience and try another *punta*.

The environment you will drive in has only 30% of the streets marked. The rest have no names, only directional arrows posted on the sides of buildings at the corners. You have entered a maze of one-way streets and no right and left turn zones. Only main streets have stop lights. The rest are unmarked and have no stop signs of any kind. These streets are up for grabs, sort of a survival of the fastest, biggest, and most aggressive. No signals are given for a right or left turn, and many of the cars you encounter will not have brake lights.

Your fellow drivers are in other cars, buses, trucks, on motorcycles or in horse drawn carts. Some move quickly, some slowly. Sometimes the slow ones are in the fast lane and the fast ones are coming up your backside in the slow lane. You will join them all on a three lane road. Prepare for the right lane, though marked "No Parking", to be blocked by parked or stalled cars. This may happen at any time. The left lane has openings in the center divider for left turns, but is not wide enough for a car attempting such a turn to pull out of the traffic lane. Your way may be blocked here by the rear end of a car, bus, truck, or even a trailer being towed by a car. And remember, no one signals ahead that he is considering such a turn, it just happens.

The center lane seems like a safe choice. Think again. The vehicles in the lanes on either side must constantly merge into this lane to avoid obstacles on either side. Remember, no one signals. And no one ever merges completely, but sort of edges over just far enough to avoid the obstacle in their lane. This produces a sort of three car squeeze in the middle lane with everyone driving partially in someone else's lane. And again…it all happens unexpectedly, no logic prevails. How are you at reading minds? Now is the time to find out.

Traffic moves either as fast as it is possible to drive, or as slow as it is possible to drive and still be considered moving. Cutting in and out of this traffic mix is to be

Virtually Real Driving

expected, and if you survive each lane change, admired by the other drivers around you. You will be cut off with inches to spare. This may even happen when there are no other cars in either of the other lanes. Now that is unexpected. Is the other driver being intentionally rude, or just unconscious of your very existence? Or is he just playing with your mind?

Let's make this a little more challenging for your driving skills. You will not be driving a zippy red sports car. You will be behind the wheel of a 20-year old VW van with manual transmission, a tendency to stall or chug in first gear and absolutely no acceleration power at all. You will be driving in an environment where the street signs, if there are any, are in a foreign language, and the light will be fading as the evening rush hour begins. Remember, your beach camp spot is somewhere on the other side of the city.

If you accepted this driving challenge and survived, you will have successfully re-lived our experience in Montevideo, the capital city of Uruguay. Or as we like to refer to it, the Ultimate Driving Experience.

> "The best way out is always through."
> Robert Frost

Chapter 44

Somewhere In Between

We left Argentina behind, taking fond memories of a huge and beautiful country with us. Ahead was Uruguay, which lay between Argentina and Brazil. Uruguay was small and mostly rural. Our first stop at *Dolores* in Uruguay confirmed our worst fears about the van and gave us some false hopes that it could be fixed in Uruguay.

Dolores was a quaint town with cobbled streets, tree lined roads and surrounding farm land. Everything had a sort of French feeling to it. The tile roofed houses sat among shade trees, turning fall colors, and rolling fields of grain and pastures sprinkled with cows. It all seemed transplanted from another continent.

The countryside was the calm before the storm. The traffic of Montevideo was the storm. This bustling city held the VW parts importer who told us that fixing the van in South America was impractical due to 30-day shipping time, and advised that we should transport the van to the US where the fix would be a slam-dunk.

Two If By Van   Karen McGinnis

Somehow we felt we had been held prisoner by our van and its constant problems throughout the whole trip. Every morning we held our breath. Would the van start? Would this be another day when Steve would lay on his back in some mud hole, wielding a heavy wrench against the sluggish starter, while I tried my best to control my emotions and start the temperamental van? But the van had also been our sanctuary. Inside was security, comfort, the familiar in a universe of unfamiliarity, unknown and discomfort. We were alternately saved and threatened by the van. We could count on it, but not too much.

Now we were cautiously edging our way through rush hour traffic in a city gone mad with driving customs we were unable to understand. We could do little but hope our transportation would hold out until we decided what to do. Should we ship it home and go on through Brazil, Venezuela and beyond with only backpacks? Or should we spend the time we needed to get replacement parts and hope the van was truly fixable, trusting mechanics we didn't know who communicated in a language we had only partially mastered, while operating in a culture we were striving to understand?

We spent eight days in Montevideo, Uruguay and in a small town nearby called *Carasco*. The trip back and forth between *Carasco* and Montevideo took about 45 minutes. Montevideo spreads along the banks of the *Rio de la Plata*, or Silver River. The Spanish named it in hopes of finding silver along its tributaries. Wrong! We found no silver there either, but did encounter some wonderful people.

We decided to follow the mechanic's advice and ship our van back to the United States. Not only would the wait for parts be long and unpredictable in its outcome, but we had learned that the roads in Brazil, the next country we would encounter after leaving Uruguay, did not connect from the border with Uruguay and the border with Venezuela. Additionally, their gasoline mixture was not consistent with our aging vehicle's need. The result of using the inappropriate gas mixture would be an additional strain on an already fragile mechanical system. We just could not handle the added risk and uncertainty generated by waiting for parts, an unknown outcome to mechanical repairs, absence of connecting roads, and bad gas.

Our first challenge in Montevideo was to arrange for the shipping of the van. Our search for a shipper was hampered by the *"mañana"* approach to business. What was critical to us was just another phone call to most of the people we called for information. We as tourists shipping a car represented a one-time-only job, with no prospects for referrals or future business. So we were, understandably at the bottom of the priority list. We hung in there, making repeatedly frustrating phone calls from public phones where street noise hampered hearing the responses we could barely understand anyway due to language differences. The computer chip phone cards we purchased at drug stores and vending machines to use on local phones often malfunctioned or cut out off in mid-sentence. Aughhh! Then of course it rained. This was lots of fun, being rained on while standing at a public phone booth on a street corner with frenetic traffic rushing by. But we located a shipper and a customs agent and a broker who seemed to work together, and ultimately with determination and patience, made the shipping of the van happen.

The eight days it took to make arrangements to ship the van were sprinkled with other experiences. Our van got "the boot" twice. The first time we had failed to buy a parking pass. We didn't know we needed one. The two previous times we had parked in Montevideo, a block attendant had approached us as we parked and taken care of the matter for us. We thought that was the normal process. This time we parked at the main plaza of the city, sat in the car for about 30 minutes while we fixed and ate our lunch, and no one approached us. The sign said "4 Hours Parking, Maximum." That was all, not a single mention of a fee, or ticket price or parking pass or anything else. Other people seemed to be parking and getting out of their cars and walking away. So we did too.

Two hours later we returned to find a bright yellow "boot" or *cepo* locked onto our rear wheel. Two passing policemen listened to our story and said they felt we did not need to pay a fine and walked us several blocks to find a pay station. All the while, one was explaining the rules and methods of the city's parking system. The private system was not connected to the transit police, but administered by a network of roving boot-men and ticket writers. It was a capitalistic free-enterprise system connected to a quasi-governmental agency through, well, a series of enforcement processes, and, needless to say, we were completely confused.

We explained our situation all over again to a pay station agent. She called the main office. We then had to walk 10 blocks to the main office for a meeting with the boss. He could not reverse the ticket, although he too felt we should not pay. An Inspector could reverse the ticket. We walked with this "boss" for several blocks to where the Inspector was meeting with other citizens on a parking matter. The Inspector then listened while the "boss" explained our plight, then pleasantly took our ticket and signed it off. A $40 fine disappeared just like that. He ordered the boot removed by cell phone and we were free.

What had really happened? We weren't completely sure. All we knew was that we hadn't paid a bribe, or the parking fine, or gone to jail. Once again, being pleasantly naïve and innocent had paid off.

That could have been the end of the story, but it wasn't. Two days later, with our parking permit firmly and properly displayed in the front window of the van, we again returned to find a boot on our wheel. Had we been targeted by the boot-men, was it harassment? We were astonished. The same friendly attitude greeted us from the traffic police at the park, who by now knew us by name. This time the boot-man and ticket writer had misread the time on the parking pass. It was good until 1500 hours and he had read it as 1300 hours. Big difference of two hours, hence the boot.

When he was contacted by our police friends, he said "No way! They just bought a new ticket to cover the time." and drove away, leaving us all frustrated and still booted. An hour later, after calls to the "boss" at the main office and verification of the error by the ticket office, the Inspector himself arrived. He looked at the ticket and our parking pass, figured out the error, realized we could not have purchased another ticket as the one we had was purchased early in the morning, exactly four hours from the 1500 hour expiration time. He signed off the ticket, asked us to excuse the bugs in the system and phoned to arrange to remove the boot. Another $40 ticket into the trash, but hours wasted and frustration experienced. We could only imagine what the work day must have been like for the "boss"' and the Inspector. Surely we were not the only ones in Montevideo who were affected by the "bugs in the system."

During our almost daily visits to this business area, we met a 22 year old transit policeman named Leonardo Botehlo. He helped us survive the stress of the boot, and made locating businesses we needed easier. In conversation, Steve learned that Leonardo was trying to learn English. Steve gave him a Spanish-English dictionary that we had carried in the van from California. We wouldn't need it any more, the van was soon to leave for the states, and the dictionary was too bulky for us to carry in our backpacks through Brazil. Besides, they spoke Portuguese in Brazil anyway. We would soon be flying into Miami, which is in a mostly English-speaking country. Leonardo was the perfect person to make use of the dictionary. He was delighted. Such books were very expensive in Uruguay, if they could be found at all. The next day he gave us some police patches as *recuerdos* or memories of our visit to Montevideo. He also hoped they would be interesting to our own policeman back home in the states, 23-year old son, Michael, with whom Leonardo now identified.

On our last day in Montevideo, we visited with Leonardo for almost an hour. We shared pictures of our family and saw pictures of his wife and baby. He explained to us that we must now speak to each other in the *'tu´* or familiar form. After all, we had exchanged gifts, shared our family pictures, talked of life, and had become friends. He explained he had wanted to have us to his home, but was afraid it was too small. We were very touched by this. We assured him that we were used to small homes, after all, we had been living in a van for the last eight months. You can't get much smaller than that. But we were leaving that day and needed to say good-by. All three of us were close to tears as we exchanged addresses and hugs and said our "somedays." His smile, twinkling eyes and sense of humor reminded us so much of Michael at home, and were a welcome ray of sunshine in our visit to Montevideo.

Other bright spots in the city were the Verig Brazilian national airline travel agent, and Rodolfo at Hernandez Travel. They both patiently helped us work out the air flights that would affordably get us from Buenos Aires to Rio de Janeiro, then through the scenic spots in Brazil, then off to Venezuela. Without their patience and skills, we would not have been able to see so many places on a budget.

The Customs agent at the Brazilian consulate also made us feel like we would be welcome in Brazil. A visa is required for US citizens to travel in Brazil. An older man, the agent had many experiences to share with us about his native country. We believed that everyone in Brazil must be as helpful as he was.

The last two people who brightened our stay in Montevideo were Carlos and Alberto. They were the caretakers at *Parador Fehardo*, where we stayed in *Carasco*. No one could accurately define a *parador*. It was a combination country restaurant, bar, barbeque, clubhouse, park area. Located on the beach, it had facilities for everything from family birthday parties to impromptu barbeques. Here we had our first *ásado* barbeque of beef ribs and chorizo sausage. The barbeque fire was made in an open cement fireplace. They burned anything that wasn't nailed down. Plywood, driftwood, scrap lumber and stumps were all thrown into the fireplace and torched with lots of gasoline. The fire roared into a towering flame and then was left to reduce itself to coals. When the coals were determined to be ready by the chef of the day, the meat was thrown on to a large metal rack that was drug over the top of the fireplace. Everything cooked at the same rate. Thin pieces were very well done and thick pieces were raw in the middle. Everything was served very hot, right off the coals. We discovered why this was the custom. As long as the meat was mouth-searing-hot, it was delicious. If you allowed it to cool slightly, it was absolutely inedible. It became tough and tasteless and greasy. We learned quickly to eat fast and not to think too much about the garbage taste of the coals which lingered on the meat.

We were also entertained by Latin drummers and baritone singers, both of which made up music on the spot for our entertainment, as we all shared barbeque. Their song reminded us that the sea and the sky are both blue and where they meet, no one knows for sure. This was their way of saying that we as visitors, and they as locals and the world in general were all one, and thankfully, all at peace. Their song about this was quite touching. Every time the baritone stood up to express a particularly poignant part of the song, the bench would tip, and a completely intoxicated grandpa who was sitting on one end would topple off into the grass. He never quite figured out how he got onto the ground, but it just didn't matter. He was having a wonderful time. That day we also shared birthday cake from a family party. It had peaches, yellow cake, caramel filling and purple frosting. It was unbelievably sweet but was actually quite good. We tasted a yellow cheese-like filling made from squash, and a wine and coke mixture that put everyone in a party mood. Such was life in Uruguay.

As we said our good-byes to Carlos, the resident manager-groundskeeper-security guard, we gave him some parting gifts. Our 220 volt heater, extension cord and plug would be of no use in Miami. The voltage was wrong for America but perfect for Uruguay. Food from our van refrigerator, including hard-to-find pickles would intrigue his taste buds. In return he gave us a battery-operated flower light. It was something to help us think of him with when we returned home. Again, we saw tears were close to the surface as he bade us have a good journey.

After loading the van into the container and once again saying goodbye to most of our worldly goods, we caught the bus to *Colonia*. This quaint town perches on a peninsula. It once defended Spanish interests along the river. The thick stone walls and stone paved streets created a charming city. From *Colonia* we rode the hydrofoil across the *Rio de la Plata* to Buenos Aires.

We spent two nights in Buenos Aries where we explored the tango culture and history of Argentina. We shared a hostel in the *Recoleta* district with a group of engineering and science students from Holland. Like most university students, they knew how to have a good time, and we got very little sleep as they visited, played cards, and watched TV until the early morning hours. It was sort of like staying in a fraternity house occupied by 12 year old boys who spoke Dutch! We evened that score when we left for our plane at 5AM. We were quiet, but the huge, open courtyard building created its own echoes. I am pretty sure that at that hour, most of the Dutch frat-boys were soundly sleeping off the party from the night before.

As the plane took off, the monument and park filled city of Buenos Aires disappeared behind us. The warm, sun-filled beaches of Brazil waited on the horizon. So began another mode of transportation on our trip to an unknown somewhere, and back. From here on out we would be traveling on public transportation and living out of our backpacks. We were no longer in a Spanish speaking country, but entering a Portuguese culture. We were traveling without the sanctuary or millstone of our van. We were alternately free and at risk. We had morphed from road trip to backpack adventure.

Copacabana

> *"She walks in beauty, like the night,
> Of cloudless climes and starry skies."*
> Lord Byron

Chapter 45

Copacabana

We traveled through Brazil on a Verig Airline Pass. It allowed us to select five destinations within Brazil and travel at a discounted rate between those points. Because it was necessary to begin the journey from certain cities outside Brazil, we had traveled from Uruguay to Buenos Aires, then had flown into Rio de Janeiro. This was our first Brazilian experience. We felt as though we had begun our trip to Latin America all over again. Here Portuguese was the national language. We got by nicely with our Spanglish as the city of Rio was an international city. They spoke English, Spanish, Portuguese, or whatever it took to communicate.

Everything that is said about Rio de Janeiro is true. There were some of the most beautiful people on earth on its beaches. Some of the women made me feel exactly like what I was, an out-of-shape American woman who had been sitting in a van for the last eight months. I was sluggish and out of shape. Of course, the men made Steve look the same way. The rippling six-packs that appeared on the beach were not for holding beer but for attracting stares and eliciting appreciation. All this was set against beaches that were wide, white and bright in the warm and welcoming sun.

Our first order of business was to find a place to stay. We were approached almost as soon as we stepped off the bus from the airport in front of the beach at Copacabana.

"¿Necesita un apartmento? Yo lo tengo. Muy grande, limpio, bonito. ¡Tambien, muy barato!"
The offer of a large, clean, and beautiful apartment for a cheap price was just too good to be true. We followed the man to the apartment, waited while he rounded up the key and permission to enter, and viewed what was an amazing space. Through the gap in the buildings in front of it you could clearly see the beach and the ocean. The price was extremely reasonable. We weren't sure if this was for real.

"What do you think? Can this place really be available? Or do you think he is just a con man waiting to take our rent money and leave us here without permission to stay the week?" I grilled Steve, remembering other times that we had almost been "had" by locals who were offering things that were too good to be true.

"We can look at some of the other places in the rental paper. Maybe we can just keep him on hold until we check them out." He replied reasonably. I couldn't decide if I liked that response, or hated it.

In the end, we looked at a couple of other places while the agent cooled his heels on the street corner. The other places didn't hold a candle to his offering. They were cramped. They smelled bad. They had no view. They were

Copacabana

up three flights of dark stairs and in a bad neighborhood. Okay, we were spoiled. We took the deluxe apartment in the sky.

After we had paid our money for the week's stay, received the keys and the pass code for the security gate, we timidly entered the apartment for the first time on our own. It seemed a little strange that we only had the keys to the servant's entrance rather than the front door, but who knew. Perhaps that was just the local custom. We also only had the use of one of the many bedrooms as that was what we had paid for. The other bedrooms were securely locked. Again, perhaps that was just the local custom.

As we prepared to go out to dinner, I could not help but run through some possible scenarios. When we returned, would the real family that lived here be sitting in the living room, watching TV, and look up, totally surprised to find two *Americanos* entering through their kitchen door? Would the security guard downstairs suddenly deny us entrance and then we would have lost our pre-paid rent, our clothes and literally be out on the street? Would we be awakened during the night to the sound of another key turning in the lock and then be held at gun point while the rental agent and his friends rummaged through our packs for valuables. Pity for them, we had nothing of value. Finding nothing, would they consider our lives expendable? We prepared for the worst. We took our passports and extra money and plane tickets with us. We locked our backpacks to the bed and locked the zippers of the packs shut. As we exited the lobby, we made sure to chat-up the security guard, played dumb while he showed us how to use the pass code, and let him know we were just going out to dinner, would be back

Two If By Van Karen McGinnis

very soon, and were not expecting any guests while we were gone. We had done all that we could.

Dinner was memorable. At a nearby restaurant, we had traditional Brazilian food. *Feijoada,* which is a stew of black beans with everything from the pig but the squeal, was served family style. While we waited for our meal to arrive, our host brought us complimentary *cachaca,* the national drink of Brazil. The white Brazilian rum promptly kicked us in the ass and made us forget any fears and uptight feelings we might have had when we entered the restaurant. I got a severe case of the giggles which delighted the restaurant owner. He sent over another round. Steve and I obliged, our faces were now flushed red and our heads were spinning. We followed the cocktails by inhaling the pork and bean stew. As we giggled and swerved our way back to our apartment, all we could think of was how much we loved Rio.

By the time we turned off the lights, we had sobered up enough to double lock the doors, put a chair tilted into the door knob and otherwise booby-trap the apartment so that anyone entering would surely wake us up. Still flushed and spinning, we drifted off to dream land, enchanted by our first night in Brazil.

During our week in Rio we did the obligatory tourist things. We shopped. We sun-tanned on the beaches. We visited the statue of Christ that overlooks the city. We went on a bus tour, stopping at the soccer stadium where Pele's skill had been cheered by thousands of his countrymen. We ate out at street-side restaurants. We cooked in and gazed at the Copacabana Beach from our living room window. We never had anything happened that indicated that we were trespassing in this apartment just one block from one of the most famous beaches in the world. We lived the life of the rich and famous on the budget of the poor and unknown. It was a week to remember.

> *"Nothing ever exists entirely alone:
> everything is in relation to everything else."*
> Siddhartha Gautama, Buddha

Chapter 46

Wet and Dry and Sandy

Our next stop in Brazil was a wet one. We flew to the border of Brazil, Argentina and Paraguay. There, where the three nation's borders met was the *Foz de Iguazu*. The giant waterfall which features the world's largest volume of water, spans the borders. The water pours out of the jungle and drops down layers of sheer rock cliffs into the river below. We took a boat ride up the river toward the base of the falls. Despite our rain gear, we were soaked by the spray from the falling water.

Buzzards circled ominously overhead. Apparently animals get caught in the current of the river upstream and are unable to avoid the plunge over the falls. The buzzards wait for the carcasses to wash up on the banks below. On one such bank, we took a break from the boat trip, dried our clothes on the rocky beach and climbed to viewing platforms. From those vantage points we could appreciate the spectacle of the masses of falling water. As far as the eye could see was swirling water, all headed inevitably toward the sheer drop-off. The jungle came right down to the water's edge on every shore. Upstream from the falls on the Brazilian side was a power plant that took full advantage of the powerful pull of the water toward the falls. The rushing water not only awed the visitor, it lit a majority of the houses in this part of Brazil.

While at *Foz de Iguazu* we stayed at a guest house. We joined some of the other visitors at a dinner show which featured the cultural dances of Brazil. Steve got into the swing of the culture as he was picked by one of the performers to join in a Samba. There on the stage, he expressed the exuberance of the day by dancing enthusiastically with a mostly nude Brazilian dancer. I was sure he was happier being picked to engage in this dance rather than joining the dance of the Pygmy head-hunters.

Our next stop in Brazil was a lot dryer and but just as exciting. The Patanal was a large section of the Amazon basin that was flooded six months of the year and dried to a desert for the other six months of the year. Luckily, we were visiting during the dry season. The roads in the Patanal were all elevated above the land to give travelers a fighting chance of making it through the area during flood season. Channels of standing water were crossed by log bridges that were held in place by posts driven into the ground. Rattling over these unstable bridges was not a confidence-inspiring experience. We sat on one bridge and counted alligators lazing in the water a few feet below. There were 34 of them that we could see from that one spot.

On a hike through the dry jungle we saw carcasses of cattle that had had close encounters with alligators and lost. There were rib cages of giant snakes lying about in the now dry fields and many, many animals such as pigs and rodents that were still alive and scampering through the underbrush.

Wet and Dry and Sandy

There were birds of every description, including large storks that stood as tall as a man and cast ominous shadows as they flew overhead. Small birds twittered in the bushes and flocks of glorious scarlet and blue macaws squawked and fought in the trees. Eagles swooped for fish in the standing water and monkeys jumped and swung and got friendly at unexpected moments.

The diversity of life was astounding. We took a horseback ride through the now dry flood plain. Termite mounds stretched up, dry now, but when the fields were flooded, the mounds reached to the top of the water. Some of the termite nests were six or ten feet high. As we got up close and personal with the Patanal, the saddle got a little too personal for my taste. My abnormally flat tail bone was rubbed raw as we ambled through the pastures and dry jungles and around crocodile infested ponds. The next week would be an uncomfortable one for me as I tried to avoid sitting on my saddle sores while on buses, planes and taxis. Life was very real in the Patanal.

Fortaleza was our next stop in Brazil. This seaport town on the north-eastern coast of Brazil gave us a taste of the lives of the local people. We visited a dance contest for school children at the cultural center. The contestants ranged from age 5 through 18. They were dressed in colorful costumes and exhibited all the enthusiasm and excitement that one might find in children anywhere. As we stood among the parents and grandparents and aunties, my eyes were wet with tears of pride for these children I didn't even know. Somehow they sensed it. Following the contest, we were surrounded, welcomed, questioned and incorporated into their celebration.

My heart was full. These children and families were just like children and families found anywhere in the world. Parents had hopes for their children. Young people had dreams. Events like this contest were opportunities for parents to celebrate their children's accomplishments and a chance for the children to feel special and enjoy their moment in the spotlight. Our chance visit was like being given a single chocolate, sweet, delightful, but insufficient. We left with a craving for more of that joy and sense of celebration.

> Q. *"What do mosquitoes eat when people or other warm-blooded animals aren't around?"*
> A. *"A large number of the world's roughly 2,000 mosquito species prefer birds, while others prefer cold-blooded critters, such as frogs."*
>
> The Wild File
> Brad Wetzler

Chapter 47

Water World

The Amazon River Basin was more than an exotic vacation destination. We discovered that it covered one-third of the surface of the country of Brazil. When you considered that Brazil was almost as large as the continental United States, you were impressed with the immensity of the Amazon region.

We first saw it from the air. Peering from the plane like awe-struck tourists, which we were, we watched as water appeared in the valleys below. Before long it seemed like there were rivers and ponds and swamps everywhere. They blended together and became the vast and muddy Amazon River. The highest elevation in the region is less than 820 feet above sea level. Most of the area is flat or even concave. Given the daily rains and huge amounts of run-off coming down from the Andes and surrounding countryside, this is a water world.

As we flew into the airport near Manaus, the Amazon

seemed more like a bay than a river. Almost nine miles from Manaus, the Solimes, or Amazon River and the Rio Negro River joined. The Rio Negro is literally black water, especially compared to the muddy brown water of the Amazon. One river is colored by the tannin from the vegetation it runs over and the other is colored by the silt from the soil. The two rivers flow side by side in the same channel without their waters mingling. For over 3 1/2 miles, there is a huge mass of water that is half brown and half black. Our guide later explained that the differences in chemical composition and water temperatures kept the waters from mixing quickly.

From Manaus, a city built in the middle of the jungle by rubber barons in the 1880's, we signed up for an extended tour of the Amazon Basin. Our tour boat headed across the Rio Negro and up the Rio Solimes. The water level was so high that we were boating past trees still standing 6 feet deep in flood waters. We had just come from the Patanal, another part of the Amazon Basin. There the dry season had already started and was gently creeping toward this flooded area. Just when it arrived and the tress had dried out, the rainy season would begin again. We tried to imagine an area this large flooding to this depth every year in the United States. It was beyond imagining.

After boating up river for two and a half hours we arrived at our floating home for the next two days. There would be no electricity and the water was either bottled or pumped from the river. While simple, the accommodations were in harmony with the jungle setting. The floating bunkhouse-hotel-and-chow hall perched on huge logs anchored in a wide part of the river. From every direction, jungle and water plants edged the lagoon. We could have been a million miles from civilization. We were surrounded on all sides by the river and the extended river basin.

This was the stuff that movies were made of. I had a flash back to the movie "Anaconda." That was not comforting. Turning away from the jungle bank, I half expected to see a pouty Katherine Hepburn motor by on the *African Queen*.

From the floating bunk house we boated out into the surrounding jungle in motorized canoes. Only six inches of freeboard separated us from the brown water of the river. In this water, now only six inches away, lurked piranhas, alligators and poisonous water snakes, huge fish the size of trucks, pink river dolphins and eels. Ducking our heads to avoid overhanging tree branches and vines, we paddled our way carefully through the flooded jungle. When not in flood stage, these openings between the trees would be foot paths. Now they were an effortless way to go deep into the jungle and feel its vibrant life.

Victoria Regina Lilies floated in the still, sunlit water. The buoyant pads opened from a spiny brown ball to become a six foot wide platform for birds, frogs and butterflies. Each leaf boasted a single white flower that measured almost a foot across. The brilliant green of the pads themselves contrasted sharply with bright red upturned edges.
Piranha fishing was next on our agenda. Unlike conventional fishing where one quietly sneaks up on the fish, piranha are attracted by violent splashing, the kind of splashing some hapless creature might make after it has fallen into the water from high in a tree. Our bait was red meat. We were excited, but a little wary of 'fishing' for piranha. In the back of our mind lurked the question of who was the predator and who was the prey.

The piranha themselves are bug-eyed fish with razor sharp teeth. Removing the hook from that mouth presented a multitude of dangers. Our native guides fearlessly grabbed not only the fish with their bare hands, but reached in among the razor sharp teeth to retrieve the hook. They must have laughed among themselves later when they remembered our reactions. Watching them was better than watching a movie thriller. Here the hero faced an element of nature that has the power to kill or maim. He was fearless in the face of danger. Here there were no fish handlers, no automated piranha and no stand-ins. It was not rehearsed. No cameras rolled. This was real.

After a candle-lit dinner (no electricity) on the floating bunk-house, half of the group went back into the darkened jungle with flashlights. From the questionable safety of the canoes they spotted the reflective eyes of alligators. Unexpectedly, the guide reached into the murky water and pulled a small alligator into the boat. Up close and personal, the alligator was no friendlier looking than the piranha had been. We were beginning to understand why the monkeys hung out in the very tops of trees, as far from the murky surface of the water as possible.
Exhausted from a day of boating and exploring the water-filled jungle, the floating camp turned into a bunkhouse filled with hanging beds. Hammocks were standard sleeping apparatus. Getting the hang of sleeping diagonally in a swinging piece of cloth was our nightly challenge. An error in calculating the correct angle would result in a sudden drop to the board floor, or a sudden twisting ride in the suspended cloth. You spent the night shaped like a banana, unable to straighten your back or roll over onto

your stomach. Unless you were an extremely sound sleeper, you awoke the next morning groggy and stiff, and not very rested.

As one of the few couples on the tour, we had the option of taking a room with a real bed. After watching the comedy of people trying to get into the hammocks and then get comfortable without falling out of the hammock, we gladly took the room. It was hot as the barge was single walled and roofed with tin, but at least the bed did not spin you unexpectedly before dropping you unceremoniously onto the floor. We also had a fighting chance against the mosquitoes that spent the night doing kamikaze-dives into the netted windows. The hammock hangers were suspended in mid-air without the benefit of netting. Their only escape from the insects was to sleep completely covered from head to toe by a sheet. That was not a comfortable prospect considering the heat and humidity.

Shortly after the generator was turned off and the lights went out, the sky began to flash with light. Heat lightening was putting on a show. Soundlessly it zipped across the sky. Reflecting on the now still waters of the lagoon, it provided a surreal backdrop to the symphony created by frogs, crickets, birds and monkeys. Each sang its own special night song to the accompanying light show above us. We had seen movies where the jungle came alive with sounds at night. It was true. Every animal called for a mate or searched for food or warded off predators or just exulted in the joy of still being alive. There was no quiet in the jungle, but there was an abundance of peace.

Then it began to rain. Lightly at first, it tinkled on the corrugated tin roof of the camp barge. Then, like the crescendo of a musical movement, it crashed down, drowning out all the other night music. Throughout the night and into the early morning, the rain fell. Only exhaustion allowed us all to sleep through the constant downpour and it's deafening drumming on the roof.

By mid morning the skies were clearing. The rising temperature and the warming sun helped to raise the humidity level as the water evaporated off of soaked tree trunks and saturated paths. In this freshly washed water world, a jungle path steaming with mist lay ahead of us. Today we would hike in the Amazon jungle.

We left our motorized canoe tied to a native jungle house on stilts. The path followed the edge of a *manioc* and pineapple field. Soon we were on a trail just wide enough to accommodate a slender person's hips. The uneven jungle growth reached out to touch us on both sides. Vines grew up from the ground and down from the trees. Some were the taproots of epiphytes or air plants that grew high in the trees. Water vines grew down from branches, sucking up water and filtering it. Roberto, our guide, cut a section off and Steve let the fresh clear water drip into his mouth. Survival made easy, if you have a sharp machete and the knowledge gained from a lifetime in the bush. We were all so hot in the humid weather. We had to wear long sleeved shirts and full length pants to avoid the mosquitoes and scratching underbrush. Being able to find water in the jungle was a worthwhile skill.

We began to see how people became lost and died in the jungle. It all looked the same to us, one tangled vine after another, one more section of bushy undergrowth, and yet another tall tree filtering the light of the sun. Staircase vines worked their way through the trees. Some were wide enough for a native to use as a stairway to the treetops. Their convoluted surfaces were also monkey friendly. These vines were a jungle highway. There was so much to know in the jungle, all of which we were ignorant to. I supposed that transplanting this knowledgeable guide to downtown anywhere would have created the same feeling of inadequacy for him.

After 15 minutes of hiking, our pants, socks and shoes were soaked. All the jungle plants were drenched from the previous night's rain. We were hot from exercising and the 80 degree temperature and the near 100% humidity. Although we were hot and sweating, we hardly noticed the discomfort as we were deep in a jungle classroom. It was filled with plants that oozed glue when scratched or boat caulk when scraped. Fruit and nuts grew on every other tree. Leafy underbrush could be used to stun fish in a river and provide abundant food. Tree bark provided quinine in case a mosquito bite was infected and malaria resulted. Our guide nodded knowingly as he pointed out this plant. He himself had had malaria five times. We began to sweat for reasons other than the heat. Would we need this malaria cure? There were mosquitoes in abundance. Which ones carried malaria? Apparently if you escaped the piranha, the alligators, the biting and stinging and burrowing insects, you just might get lucky. You might only come down with a case of malaria as a memento of your visit to the Amazon.

The guide showed us how a broken stem could provide a milk of magnesia-like substance. The crushed leaves of other plants smelled and tasted like spearmint, Vicks Vapor-rub or garlic. The jungle was a storehouse of food, medicine and usable materials.

This was the reason so many people supported with vigor the efforts to save the rain forests of the world. They certainly were places filled with answers, some to questions which had not even been formulated.

After hiking into the jungle for an hour, we turned and retraced our steps. Then the rain began again. Here under the jungle canopy, we were hardly affected. Our rain jackets were already wet to the shoulders from the overhanging vegetation. The few drops that fell through the leaves above us were almost refreshing on our hot faces.

Luck was with us and the sun began to shine as we pushed off in our canoe. Our visit to the jungle had been filled with water in one form or another. We had floated on it, slept over it, walked in it, drank it from vines and worn it from head to toe. The immensity of the lessons in the Amazon water-world had touched us and nourished our imagination and our senses.

> *"If you have something of importance to say,
> for God's sake, start at the end!"*
> Sarah Jeannette Duncan

Chapter 48

The Beginning of the End

This was the beginning of the end of our trip. We arrived in Venezuela from Brazil by way of refrigerated bus. Most of the passengers on board had brought their sleeping bags or blankets with them to compensate for the over-cooled interior of the "first class" bus that took us from Boa Vista, Brazil, to Venezuela. Our only explanation for the enthusiasm with which the driver cranked up the AC was that he must have felt he was giving us our money's worth. After all, we had purchased a ticket specifically for an "air conditioned bus." These buses were not only air conditioned, they were refrigerated. Our alternative was to ride economy class. These buses would have been filled with locals, farm animals, vegetables and market goods. They had stiff, non-reclining seats and barely operable windows. We would have been more than hot, we would have been stifled. We took the lesser of the two evils, and bought tickets for the refrigerated bus. We were grateful that we had our sleeping bags with us in our backpacks.

The bus was so cold that the windows iced over where the air conditioner blew against the glass. We zipped our sleeping bags up to our noses, leaving only a small hole through which to breathe and gain a partial peek at the passing countryside. Here in Venezuela, even the bus rides brought home the differences between rich and poor. The poor were hot, stinky, crowded and treated like cattle. Those with a little more money were only slightly better off as they struggled to survive the refrigerated passage through the countryside, completely at the mercy of the non-responsive and non-empathetic bus driver. Perhaps only the *uber*-rich reached a level that provided some semblance of comfort. As we thought about all the dangers that existed in this country from kidnappers and paparazzi, we doubted that even they were all that comfortable, even in their chauffeur-driven cars and private planes. We had plenty of time to think about all these things as we shivered our way across northern Brazil and into Venezuela.

One of Venezuela's premier tourist attractions was the *Salto Ángel*, or Angel Falls, the world's tallest waterfall. It was located deep in the *tauney* or mesa area of southeastern Venezuela. A *tauney* was a flat topped mountain with nearly vertical sides. No roads led to *Canaima*, the closest village to the falls. For us, this meant a 45 minute flight in a four-seat, single engine plane. The plane trip provided a view of the jungle and water-filled delta landscape that surrounded *Canaima*. We were lucky and flew in a plane that carried only the pilot, a "lumper" or freight handler, and us. Some of our traveling companions were not so lucky. They were traveling in the company of sides of pork, bunches of bananas, sacks of potatoes, and the multitude of flies and smells that accompany a plane load of groceries.

The handlers for the planes had tried to separate Steve and me, placing me in one of the cramped seats next to a huge

The Beginning of the End

bunch of bananas. The tears rolling down my face and the fact that I was already hyperventilating encouraged them to move me to the plane that Steve was riding in. My place was taken by a new friend, an East Indian traveler. He promptly lost his lunch out the plane window upon landing. His experience made us thankful our only wet-palm-moments were related to flying through the fringes of towering thunderheads, and the white-knuckle gripping of plane seats as we made the classic and bumpy jungle landing at the tiny airfield at *Canaima*.

The *Salto Ángel* experience really began at the lagoon that fronted the spectacular waterfalls of *Sapo* and *Sapito*. They fell into a tranquil lagoon that spread out into the jungle. Palm trees and pink sand lined the edges. From the top of these falls the meadows, palms trees and surrounding jungle looked like the backdrop from another Michael Crichton screenplay, somewhere between *Jurassic Park* and *Lost World*. The vegetation was classic dinosaur delight.

Sapo Falls was a huge fall in itself. If *Salto Ángel* had not been the reason for people to come to this area, Sapo Falls itself would have been a justifiable tourist attraction. Volumes of water cascaded over the sheer rock cliffs after gathering in the jungles above and rushing over white water rapids. The biggest treat at these falls was the opportunity to walk behind them. The guides told you that you would get wet. They didn't tell you that you would get soaked to the skin. There was a rope or pipe handrail built into the eroded cave area just behind the tons of cascading water. As water poured down around you, you gingerly picked your way along the wet slippery rocks, squealing and screaming as you walked the whole length of the falls. If you were lucky, you didn't get behind a grandmother-type who was scared to death and shell-shocked by the experience. This definitely slowed down the passage. Some people became so scared, they were frozen to the spot and had to be rescued by guides or family members. After reaching the other side and taking the requisite photos of yourself, soaked to the skin in front of the falls, you had to work your way back along the same path to where you had left your towel and dry clothes. You left them there where it was dry if you were smart, that is.

Reaching *Salto Ángel* itself was not an easy process. Two hours of riding in a leaky motor-driven boat took you to the first camp. The boats leaked at every joint. They rode low in the water and were hand made. Despite their leaky condition and shallow freeboard, they must fight their way upstream against the current. Every fiber of the boat was put to the test. Your life was in the hands of the pilot who sat at the back controlling the motor and of the assistant "boat monkey" who was perched at the bow. He sat at the front of the boat and watched for submerged logs and rocks. Periodically he ran to the back of the boat and bailed frantically to empty the boat of water that had seeped into it through the cracks or splashed into it from the waves as the boat fought its way up the rapids. No one was watching for logs or rocks when he was bailing and no one was bailing when he was watching. There must have been some system of prioritizing the dangers. Was it wiser to keep the boat above water by bailing or to keep the boat above water by watching for logs or rocks?

One set of rapids was so rough that the Venezuelan government has declared them unsafe for tourists. The boats let you off and went through them empty, then picked you up further upstream. Your only means of reaching the

The Beginning of the End

pick-up point was to walk. This sounds easy enough, except for the attack of the midges along the way. These almost unseen critters must have huge mouths as the locals called them *"boca grande"* which means "big mouth" in Spanish. They made a tiny blood-red hole in your skin which usually itched like crazy later that day, developed a red and then yellow ring, and continued to itch for days to come. We had encountered them before in the jungles of the Amazon and had read warnings in the travel guides. We were prepared with long pants, long sleeve shirts and insect repellant. It was hot walking through the tropical sun in long pants and long sleeve shirts, but the poor innocents who had not prepared themselves experienced over a dozen bites on a single calf. Agony followed for them as the blood dripped down their legs and the bites began to swell even as we loaded up the boats on the other side of the rapids.

Camp for the first night consisted of a huge open-air tin-roofed shed. It was filled with hammocks strung from the rafters. This would be our home for two days. Here in an unlit kitchen the cook prepared our food over propane burners. There was no electricity, toilets were flushed by dumping in a bucket of water, and the showers didn't leave you "clean" as the water came directly from the river. People with insect bites were beginning to realize that their agony had just begun. Their bites swelled and began to itch. Scratching just made the itching worse. Topical ointments did nothing to quell the irritation. Their discomfort would last into the week ahead. Once again, the memento of the jungle stayed with you, a thing to remember. Some sufferers tried to numb the pain by drinking whatever alcoholic beverage presented itself and then escape into sleep. The result of this treatment was that the next day found them itching and with a nasty headache.

Two If By Van   Karen McGinnis

As we relaxed after the first evening's meal, I was not all that surprised to see a huge rat run across the open ceiling of the kitchen, cross the dining area and run down a slanting drain pipe before disappearing into the jungle. We won't even talk about the bugs that made the shed and the jungle their home. Better not to think about some things. We just ate our food, sight unseen in the half-light from candles and lanterns. We endured a restless night as we tried to get comfortable in the hammocks, ignored our aching backs, bug bites, lack of oxygen as we tried to breathe through clothes laid over our faces to ward off mosquitoes and prayed that no rat or bat dropped on us during the night. Morning did not come quickly.

The second day required that we take another two hour boat ride upstream. Today we could see the spectacular mesas called *tauneys* that would be the home to *Salto Ángel*. These sheer cliff mesas rose sharply out of the jungle, and were laced with dozens of small falls. They were the home to unique collections of plants and animals that lived out their lives isolated in the jungles on the tops, unable to leave or access other groups of flora or fauna. Many mesas had never been explored, let alone studied for possible new species of plant or animal life. There were so many places on our trip where man had not walked or changed the natural order of things.

We beached our leaking boats at the next jungle camp. An hour and a half hike through the jungle lay ahead of us. This required the crossing of streams that interlaced the steep hillside. The roots of strangler figs provided footholds as we climbed the steep trail. The frequent rains made the exposed rocks, roots and soil slippery and moss covered. A careless footstep could easily result in a nasty

The Beginning of the End

fall and an unexpected injury. We were four hours by boat from the nearest village and a very long and steep trail now separated us from the spot where the boats were beached. After the four hour boat ride there was still a 45 minute flight in a small plane over trackless jungle to reach the nearest real doctor. We walked carefully, planting each foot, moving our walking sticks and paying attention to what we were doing. Losing focus here could mean losing more than your way. We walked as though our lives depended on each foot step.

After an hour we reached an overlook. Here, perched on rocks, we could see *Salto Ángel* ahead of us. The falls were almost a kilometer high. One kilometer equaled .62 of a mile or 3,280 feet. From this vantage point, the top was hidden in the clouds, and the bottom was still obscured in the jungle. We had another half an hour of climbing before reaching the base of the falls.

The base of the falls was strewn with large boulders that had tumbled from the sheer rock cliffs. Pools formed amid the boulders. The falls were so high that the only way to see the entire falls from this close was to lie flat on one of the boulders and gaze upward. As we did so, the breeze high on the cliffs shifted the clouds and the full length of the falls was exposed. It was spectacular. A tall ribbon of white water appeared at the edge of the jungle-covered cliff above, and fell for what seemed like forever toward the spot where we lay. We were lucky to have a full stream of water that could be seen falling the whole length of the falls. In the dry season, the falls were a trickle and disappeared into a mist about half way down the cliff face. The six hours of rain we had had the night before had swollen the falls considerably and now it fell in splendor to the rocks and pools below.

After enjoying the view of the falls and the view of other falls far across the jungle valley, we rested on the sunny rocks, swam in the cool water of the pools and then began our long hike back down the root and rock-covered path. Reaching *Salto Ángel* had been one of the goals of our trip. The spectacle of the falls made the journey to reach it well worth the effort. Ahead of us lay the leaky boat ride down the river, the overnight at *Camaina*, the 45 minute small plane ride over the jungle, and then another refrigerated bus ride farther into Venezuela. It was the beginning of the end.

> *"Truth is shorter than fiction."*
> Irving Cohen

Chapter 49

Leaving It All Behind

It didn't seem possible, but we had arrived at the end of our adventure. At least we were at the end of the adventures we had planned. We left the tiny plane that had flown us to visit Angel Falls behind and boarded yet another refrigerated bus. Two, day-long trips by refrigerated bus brought us to Caracas, Venezuela. We arrived at the airport in plenty of time to catch our plane and even did a little shopping. I had restrained myself throughout the trip and had bought very little in the way of souvenirs or "tourist crap". We had been traveling in the van in which every square inch was carefully packed. Collecting souvenirs was something that was done cautiously and with consideration of the space available. We were also traveling on a budget. I would rather have had the money for the flight home or emergency van repairs than purchase a piece of the local culture. My memories were not susceptible to rust or moths or mold and could not be stolen. They took up very little space.

At the airport, in a jewelry store, I found a topaz, diamond and gold ring. It was subtle and the price was right. It almost fit. My fingers were swollen from carrying my heavy pack. Or perhaps it was from sitting in a refrigerated bus for two days, barely sleeping in questionable rooms and eating food that was not familiar and prepared by unknown hands. For whatever reason, the ring was too tight. It was, however, the perfect symbol of the trip. The topaz had been mined in Venezuela and the small diamonds were also from the region. The design was distinctively South American and the gold was of a karat weight not found in the United States. Just as we resigned ourselves to not buying the ring, the salesperson had a brilliant idea. This particular jewelry store had a counterpart in Miami. We were going to Miami on this flight. They would mail it and we could drop by their store in Miami and pick it up later after it had been sized. The problem was solved. Measurements were taken, addresses and dates were given and payment made. It would be a life-long reminder of our trip. This seemed especially appropriate a symbol as we were planning on celebrating a specific event with Steve's family when we arrived in the States. We were getting married. This ring would tie together this shake-down trip with the rest of our lives together.

After the time spent arranging for the ring to be shipped and sized, we rushed to the boarding gate to catch our plane. We discovered it had been delayed indefinitely due to engine trouble. "Better to be delayed than crashed" quickly became our motto. Many of our fellow passengers were not of the same opinion about the "delayed" part and there were many loud conversations between the non-communicative airline representatives and the now too-late-for-connecting-flight-passengers. Small groups of passengers would approach the ticket agents as they realized that the time for making their next connection was approaching. They demanded answers. No answers were given. Gesturing angrily and obviously unhappy, group after group was turned away dissatisfied. We had learned over the last year to just chill. It would be what it would be. Either we would get there, or we would get there later. High blood pressure and loud aggressive encounters never seemed to solve problems. We began to feel as though we were sitting in the audience, watching a show play out on the stage before us. Our tickets from Caracus to Miami were purchased. Now it was the airline's responsibility to make them good. The worst that could happen was that we would be put up for the night in a hotel, or be put on a later flight. Either way, no one was waiting for us in Miami, and one more night in South America was fine with us.

Eventually all the passengers were herded onto a sort of moving fuselage, an airplane mock-up without engine or wings, just seats. In this strange apparition, partly bus and partly plane, we were shuttled to another part of the airport. There, in the back lot of the airport, we were loaded onto a parked plane. We were on our way to our connection in Bogotá, Columbia. We were now two hours late. The plane was filled with passengers who had missed connections to flights going all over Central and South America, the Caribbean and North America. What a logistical nightmare it must have been for the airline. Of course, everyone was extremely tired, stressed and unhappy. Voices were loud, people were crabby and children cried. To make the situation even more uncertain, none of the airline representatives were giving out information about how everyone's problems were going to be solved. No one really knew for sure what was to become of us or how we were going to get to our destinations. Rumors were rampant.

Two If By Van Karen McGinnis

The city of Bogotá and the country of Columbia both had reputations among travelers. We had intentionally avoided the country when we shipped our van from Panama to Ecuador. We had met residents of Columbia who recommended we NOT visit the country. Every guide book advised travelers to visit with extreme caution. Now we were about to land in the capital city of Bogatá with no place that we knew of to stay, and no concrete idea of how we were going to get from Bogatá to Miami.

After another cattle-like experience in the Bogatá airport, we were herded into buses. We all had only our carry-on luggage and no idea of where we were going or what was going to happen to us. Again, this was fine with us as we only had our backpacks with us and were on no set schedule. The airline representatives were noticeably mute. The rumor among the passengers was that there would be no flights out of the city that night. We were to spend the night in Bogotá as guests of the airline. These were rumors, because the airline representatives were very close-mouthed about the whole situation. They avoided answering direct questions, and even became non-responsive to native Spanish speakers who were demanding to know what was going on. The idea that we were in some strange movie kept popping into my mind. We were in no real hurry to arrive in Miami, so just kept our mouths shut and sat quietly in the back of the bus.

We were driven in a caravan of shuttle buses through the heart of Bogotá. The city itself seemed normal enough. It was on a high plateau surrounded by mountains. The streets seemed orderly, the parks green and the businesses and houses were within normal range for South America. So what had all the fuss in the guide books been about? We

Leaving It All Behind

soon found out. Upon close observation, we began to notice pairs of army men or police guards on street corners. They all held rifles or submachine guns at the ready. When an armed man is not expecting much to happen, he can sling his gun over his shoulder. These men carried their guns in-hand and pointed outward toward the streets as though expecting the worst to happen at any moment. Fortunately for us, the worst turned out to be just seeing the armed guards. No violence ever erupted.

Our shuttle bus arrived at the Don Humbolt Hotel, a huge glass and chrome, five star establishment. After more confusion in the lobby with arriving airline guests jockeying for rooms, we were escorted by a bellhop to our gorgeous room, complete with king bed, huge bathroom, hairdryer, and many deluxe amenities. We were going to spend the last night in a lot more luxury than we had known cumulatively during the whole trip. Our stay also included a buffet dinner and breakfast. We felt like we had just hit the jackpot and this must be Las Vegas. We spent some time congratulating each other on our situation, made some "cha-ching" noises, and taking staged photos in our room. After a delightful dinner in the downstairs dining room, we asked the concierge what would be the best way for us to take an evening walk and see the city. Everyone behind the desk looked at us as though we had lost our minds. There was no best way to take a walk when armed police guarded every street corner. Walking after sunset was unwise and probably violated some curfew or other that was imposed on the city. We were advised in no uncertain terms to return to our rooms and be glad we were in such a beautiful and safe place. We never tried the front doors, but I can almost guarantee that they were locked from the inside.

Two If By Van — Karen McGinnis

We were a little unnerved when we realized that the day we would fly from Bogotá to Miami was Friday the 13th. We swallowed hard, loaded ourselves and our backpacks onto the plane and took off. Destination: Miami, Florida, the United States of America and freedom from armed guards and uncertainty. Our trip to Central and South America had been an experience from the first moment. Our last moments in Bogotá had maintained that level of unexpected excitement.

In Miami we still had to retrieve our van after it had spent six weeks in a sweat-box being shipped from Uruguay. Customs, EPA, DEA and other unknown agencies awaited us. Then there was the nagging problem of fixing the poorly running van, then driving it across 10 states to reach California. Somewhere in the back of our imagination, we knew our adventure was not yet over.

> *"You may marry the man of your dreams, but fifteen years later you're married to a reclining chair that burps."*
> — Roseanne Barr
>
> *"We are not even CLOSE to being married for 15 years, and I don't own a reclining chair."*
> — Steve Frayer

Chapter 50

Home Again, Home Again

After all our experiences in Central and South America, Miami seemed tame. We rented a car at the airport and found a hotel. We retrieved our van from the freight yard where the hardest part was watching the struggle of a too-plump dockworker try to squeeze into the van that was parked inside the shipping container. Steve offered to drive it out, and while that violated the longshoreman's union rule, they agreed. We missed all the red tape threatened by travel guides and previous travelers' accounts and sailed through customs. We had nothing to declare. They took one look at the inside of our van and decided that a search was unwise. After six weeks in the shipping crate, the inside was covered in a fine film of mold. Washing everything in Clorox was a small price to pay to have it safely back on American soil. We made the van a promise that it could rust in peace back home in Maui if it would please, just make it there.

The valve trouble we had had in Argentina and Uruguay still haunted us. While our van engine was again repaired in Miami, we spent a week at the beach in a timeshare we exchanged for the one we had bought while having the van fixed in Mazatlan. That seemed like so long ago. We visited family. We picked up our wedding ring at the jewelers in Miami. We found a ring for Steve, which of course, did not fit and had to be resized and sent to Tennessee where we would be married at a family reunion. We might have made it back to the United States, but there were still rocks in the road.

After driving our now repaired van through Georgia, South, then North Carolina and into Tennessee, we met family at the reunion in Gatlinburg. Steve had arranged our wedding over the internet. It was held at a small chapel in the Smokey Mountains. His family was taken by surprise at this invitation. What had originally just been admiration for our courage and determination at attempting and succeeding in completing a continental circumnavigation, turned into appreciation for the fact that, at last, someone was going to marry their 40-year old quirky son and brother.

The wedding was small, intimate and picturesque. There were a few twists and turns in the road as you drove through "Butcher Hollow" to get to the chapel. We spent one night in a mountain cabin as a token honeymoon. We still had to drive across the United States to get back to California and then fly back to our new home in Maui, Hawaii.

We had left Maui on September 16, 2000. We returned on September 15, 2001, just 4 days after September 11, and almost exactly one year after we had left the island. During that time we had traveled by land, sea, air, on foot, by bus, taxi, shuttle, van, train, reed boat, canoe, and speed boat. We had passed through 16 separate countries, not including crossing the United States from coast to coast. We had been in high places and low places. We had sweated in wet hot places and shivered in cold dry places. We had seen thunder, lightning, rain, snow, fog, sunshine and smog. We had viewed life at its best and at its most troubling.

The biggest journey we had taken had not been in the physical world. We had traveled far in the spiritual and emotional world. Here we had hit the highs and lows of our individual and collective strengths. We had seen the best of ourselves and the worst of ourselves. We had traveled to the end of the road, inside and out and come home the better for it. Or at least, we had come home!

Aloha, as the Hawaiians say, may the breathe of God be with you.

Steve Frayer and Karen McGinnis

Index

A

Acapulco, 39, 60
Alaska, 232
Almirante Nieto Mountain, 237
Amazon River, 275, 276, 282, 283, 289
anarchy, 16
Angel Falls, 286, 293
Antarctic, 232
Antigua, Guatemala, 106, 107
Argentina, 220, 222, 223, 224, 245, 246, 253, 262, 271, 302
Arequipa, Peru, 195, 199
Arizona, USA, 225
Atacama Desert, 201, 202, 203, 206, 208

B

Bahia Ensenada, 233
Beagle Channel, 233
Belize, 70, 75, 77, 78, 79, 129
Belize City, Belize, 74, 76, 78 Big
Sur, California, 60
Boa Vista, Brazil, 285
Body Snatchers, 35, 36, 37, 38
Bogatá, Columbia, 295, 296, 297, 298
Brazil, 24, 25, 253, 254, 255, 258, 260, 262, 265, 268, 271, 272, 273, 275, 285
Buenos Aires, Argentina, 219, 259, 262, 265

C

California, 215, 239, 243, 258, 299, 302 Campeche, Mexico, 61

Canada, 127, 164
Canaima, Venezuela, 286, 287, 292
Cape Horn, 219
Capitola, California, 57
Caracas, Venezuela, 293, 295
Carasco, Uruguay, 254, 260
Cascabela, Mexico, 19, 21
Caulker Cay, Belize, 77
Cayo District, Belize, 78
Cedona, Honduras, 119, 120
CentralAmerica, 108, 112, 129, 157, 186, 211, 295, 298, 301
Cerro Sombrero, Argentina, 227, 228, 229
Chacabuco, 220, 222
Chan Chan, Peru, 177
Chichen Itza, 115
Chile, 199, 200, 201, 202, 211, 214, 215, 220, 222, 224
Choluteca, Honduras, 123, 126
Chultun Ruins, 115
clothes, clothing, 4, 5, 6, 7, 16
Coyhaique, 222
Colca Canyon, Peru, 207
Colombia, SA, 143, 144, 296
Colima, Mexico, 60
Colonia, 262
Copacabana, Brazil, 265, 266, 269
Copan, Honduras, 117, 118
Costa Blanca, Peru, 171
Costa Rica, Central America, 100, 130, 132, 137, 144
Cusco, Peru, 195, 196, 197, 198

D
Darian Gap, 26, 144
Dolores, Uruguay, 253

E
Easter Island, 117
Ecuador, SA, 144, 151, 154, 161, 163, 164, 165, 166, 171
Edzna, 115
Esmarelda, Colombia, 25
Equator, 151

F
Fernando Magullan, 232
Food, 7, 8, 9, 10, 15, 30
Fortaleza, Brazil, 273
Foz de Iguazu, 271, 272
Fruitillar, Chile, 212, 213

G
Galápagos, 185, 186, 189
Garifuna, 104
Gatlinburg, Tennessee, 302
Georgia, USA, 302
Guatemala, Guatemalan, 82, 83, 87, 91, 97, 100, 105, 106, 109, 111, 118, 129
Guayaquil, Ecuador, 150, 151, 158, 162, 163, 165
Guerrero, Mexico, 60
Gulf of Mexico, 60, 61

H
Hacienda Guiliaguime, Cholutca, Honduras, 123
health issues, 13,14,15
Hernando Magallanes, 232
Honduras, 105, 118, 120, 129
Huatulco, 60
Huayna Picchu, Peru, 193
Humberstone, Chile, 208
Humbolt Current, 187
Hurricane Mitch, 1998, 124

I
iguanas, 24, 25
Incas, 191, 192, 193, 196, 199
Isla Ballestas, Peru, 186, 189
Isle de Flores, Guatemala, 103
Isthmus of Tehuantepec, Mexico, 58, 60
Ixtapa, Mexico, 60

J
jewelry, 16

K
Kabah, 115

L
La Alameda, Quito, Ecuador, 152
Lago Arenal, 133
Lago Buenos Aires, Argentina, 222
Lago General Carrera, Chile, 222, 223
Lago Izabal, Guatemala, 97
Lago Llanquihue, Chile, 212
Lago Pahoe, 239

Lago Tinquilco, Chile, 216 Lake
Petan Itza, Guatemala, 91 Lake
Titicaca, Peru, 195
Lake Yaxha, Guatemala, 87, 88, 94
Las Palmas, Panama, 25
Latin America, 23, 37, 100, 105, 146, 171, 173, 186
   207, 211, 265
laundromats, 6
Lima, Peru, 181, 182
Livingston, Guatemala, 104 Lo
de Marcos, Mexico, 60 Los
Lagos Park, 133
Los Mochis, Mexico, 29

M
MachuPicchu, Peru, 191, 192, 193, 194
Manaus, Brazil, 275, 276
Manzanillo, Panama, 161
Masaya Volcano, Nicaragua, 130
Maui, Hawaii, 63, 88, 301, 302, 303
Mayan Ruins, 105, 117
Mazatlán, Mexico, 35, 38, 39, 40, 42, 60, 61, 302
medications, 14, 106
Mexico, Mexican, 21, 22, 23, 29, 30, 31, 38, 39, 40, 41,
   43, 44, 47, 48, 49, 51, 53, 58, 59,   60, 61, 67, 71,
   75, 105, 112, 115,   116, 117, 118,   127, 129, 157
Mexico City, Mexico, 42
Miami, Florida, USA, 258, 262, 294, 295, 296, 298, 301,
   302
Michoacán, Mexico, 60
Mochi, 172, 173
money, 17,18
Montevideo, Uruguay, 251, 254, 255, 259

Mr. Morro's RV Resort, Mexico, 29

N
Nayarit, Mexico, 60
Nepal, 239
New Jersey, USA, 100
Nicaragua, Central America, 129, 130
North Carolina, USA, 302

O
Olmec, 116
Ornas Tribe, 232
Oxaca, Mexico, 60

P
Pacific Ocean, 60
Palacio Gobierno, Quito, Ecuador, 152
Palenque, 115
Pampagrande, Peru, 173, 174
Panama, Central America, 143, 144, 146, 163, 167, 296
Panama City, Panama, 145, 147, 148
Pan American Highway, 26, 202
Paracus, Peru, 185, 186, 208
Parado Fehardo, Uruguay, 260
Paraguay, South America, 271
Parque El Ejido, Quito, Ecuador, 151, 155
Parque Nacional de Tierra Del Fuego, 232
Patagonia, 219, 225
Patanal, 272,273, 276
Peru, SA, 170,171, 176, 177, 181, 199, 201, 202
Petan, Guatemala, 87
picaduras, 30
Playa las Glorias, 29

Plaza de Independencia, Quito, Ecuador, 15
prescriptions, 14
Primavera Province, Argentina, 227
Pucon, Chile, 216, 217
Puerto Escondido, Mexico, 55, 57
Puerto Montt, Chile, 219
Puerto Natales, 219, 236
Puerto Vallarta, Mexico, 47
Puno, Peru, 195
Punto Raton, Honduras, 119

Q

Quintana Roo, Mexico, 61
Quiroga, Honduras, 117
Quito, Ecuador, 151, 154, 155, 158, 161, 162, 163, 165

R

Radatilly, Argentina, 246
refrigeration,   9
re-hydration, 9, 10
RincóndelaVieja, 130, 132, 137
Rio de Janeiro, Brazil, 259, 265
Rio de la Plata, Uruguay, 254, 262
Rio de Paine, 236
Rio Dulce, Guatemala, 97, 98, 100, 102, 104
Rio Negro, 276
Rio Simpson National Park, Chile, 222
Ruta Maya, 105, 112, 113, 115, 116, 117

S

safety, 16, 17, 18
Salto Angel, 286, 287, 288, 290, 291, 292
San Andreas, Guatemala, 91, 97
San Diego, California, 100
Santa Cruz, California, 55, 57, 71
Sapito Falls, 287
Sapo Falls, 287
Sayil ruins, 173
Selkman Tribe, 232
shots, 14
Sierra Madre Mountain Range, 59
Sinaloa State, Mexico, 60
Sipan, Peru, 173
Solimes River, 276
SouthAmerica, 43, 143, 149, 165, 185, 186, 211,
    219, 222, 243, 249, 294, 295, 298, 301
South Carolina, USA, 302
Spanish, 31, 43
Strait of Magullan, 235
Santiago, Chile, 239

T

Tamarugal, National Reserve, Chile, 204 Tennessee, USA, 302
Tepic, Mexico, 39, 40, 41, 42, 43, 44, 47
Tibet, 239
Tierra Del Fuego, 83, 219, 220, 227, 229, 231, 232, 233,
    235
Tikal, Guatemala, 88, 105, 106, 109, 110, 111, 112
Torres del Paine, 235, 244

Torres Glaciar, 237
Tulum, 117

U

Ushuaia, 232
United Status, 127, 199, 255, 275
Urubamba River, 191
Uruguay, Uruguayans, 243, 251, 253, 254, 255, 258, 261, 265, 298, 302
Uxmal, 115

V

vehicle maintenance, 10, 11, 12
Venezuela, 254, 255, 259, 285, 286, 289, 292, 294
Veracruz, Mexico, 61
Villahermosa, Mexico, 116
Villarrica, Chile, 211
VolcanArenal, Costa Rica, 130, 133, 135
Volcan Orsorno, Chile, 213

W

washing clothes, 6
water, 9, 10, 30

x

Xlapak, 115

Y

Yaxha, Guatemala, 117
Yucatán Península, Mexico, 61